BEYond hOrroR HOloCAusT

A Deeper Shade of Red

CHas. baLUN

BEYOND HORROR HOLOCAUST
A DEEPER SHADE OF RED

CHAS. BALUN

Fantasma
BOOKS

aCknoWLedGemEntS

GRATEFUL THANKS TO ERIC CAIDIN OF HOLLYWOOD BOOK AND POSTER CO. FOR HIS KINDNESS, PATIENCE AND GENEROSITY IN ALLOWING ME ACCESS TO HIS PHOTO FILES. HIS COLLECTION HAS PROVIDED THIS BOOK WITH ALL THE SPLATTER THAT MATTERS. BLOODY THANKS, MY FRIEND.

THANKS TO SHAWN SMITH FOR BEING A RIGHTEOUS BLOOD BROTHER AND VERY SPECIAL THANKS TO ROBERT MARRERO, TRUE BELIEVER, FOR KEEPING THE FAITH.

ADDITIONAL PHOTOS PROVIDED BY THE DEEP RED ARCHIVES AND FANTASMA BOOKS.

DEDICATED TO LUCIO FUCI. REST IN PEACE, MAESTRO.

CONTENTS

MICHAEL MEYERS - 25 YEARS OF *Halloweens*.

INTRODUCTION

*"I approach madness as something dangerous and I'm afraid,
but I also want to go to it, to see what's there...to embrace it."*

Dario Argento (1991)

"A good scare is worth more to a man than good advice."

Edgar Watson Howe (1911)

Welcome to my nightmares, dear friends. Within these pages, we'll celebrate the simple, unfettered joy that various beasts, bad-assed masked psychos, alien carnivores, radiated mutants, cannibals, zombies and power-tool abusers have brought to us over the years. Though the horror film has, of course, undergone a plethora of changes since Thomas Edison's early take on *Frankenstein* nearly a century ago, the beast remains much the same. It wants to scare the living hell out of you...or die trying. The horror film wants to make you squirm and cry for your mommy. It wants to take you places you just might not want to go, show you things you were, perhaps, never meant to see. But still, the sometimes lethal mix of dread and daring sets your foot squarely on that slippery, sanguineous welcome mat, perched precariously close to the edge of an abyss.

"The oldest and strongest emotion of mankind is fear," wrote H.P. Lovecraft. "And the oldest and strongest kind of fear is fear of the unknown." In *Lord Jim (1930)*, author Joseph Conrad, no stranger himself to man's heart of darkness, asked, "How does one kill fear, I wonder? How do you shoot a spectre, slash off its spectral head or take it by its spectral throat?" Horror is as ancient as it is elusive. Fear is the engine that drives the horror film. We are all afraid of different things, to be sure, but buried deep within us all lies a common dread: death, pain, disease, disfigurement, the loss of a loved one. In odd and

unusual ways, the horror film allows us glimpses of these catastrophic terrors, but also permits us to escape and survive them at the end. In a very cathartic sense, these films show us how to stay strong and how to beat back the beasts that threaten to eat us alive.

Through a long and grand cinematic tradition, the horror film has asked the really tough questions and proposed the most grisly of fates for the unbeliever. Still frequently flagellated by the "serious press," relegated to minor league status by mainstream cinema and often used as a convenient whipping boy by trendy moralists, the horror film perseveres. It's dark, deadly talons are simply buried far too deep in our very ancient souls to ever allow an easy escape.

In 1986, the now-defunct FantaCo Enterprises in New York published one of my very first books, *Horror Holocaust*, and I assumed the role of a rather giddy guide on a macabre tour through a freakish sideshow of beasts, bugs, bloodletting and things that go splat in the night. It was my opportunity to both embrace and pontificate on the kind of films that I'd loved since I was a kid, as well as introduce fledgling travelers to my very own Vault of Horror. Now, a decade and-a-half later, I'm certainly older, yet perhaps no wiser. I still love horror films--even the really shitty ones--with a skewed passion and an unfathomable devotion known only to the real diehards. I still eagerly seek out and attempt to replicate the prickly sensations I first felt when I saw *King*

Kong, *Godzilla* or *Frankenstein Meets the Wolfman* on local television for the very first time. Or, relive again, the edgy foreboding that accompanied a midday double-bill of *Torso* and *The Texas Chainsaw Massacre* at the local multiplex. I still yearn for what I felt that rainy night in 1983, well after midnight at the Los Angeles Film Expo, when I waited in a long line of the faithful for the West Coast premiere of Sam Raimi's *The Evil Dead*. I want the epiphany repeated, again and again, of what I experienced the first time I saw Peter Jackson's swaggering chunkblower, *Braindead*. That elusive, ephemeral vibe rarely returns, but certainly not for lack of trying.

In this all new, never-before-published collection, I want to revisit and renew the original spirit and intent of the *Horror Holocaust* of years past.

So, let this volume again be a celebration of the wet, the wild and the unspeakably horrific nightmares conjured up by the legions of talented directors, writers, actors, special effects artists and True Believers who have managed to scare the living shit out of us for nearly a century.

And God bless 'em for that!

Here's Blood (and a 14" splinter) in Yer Eyeball!
Chas. Balun, Summer 2003

INDUSTRIAL STRENGTH LOBOTOMY, *Gates of Hell* STYLE.

HE LICKS IT...THE FLICK BITES IT.
Zombie Island Massacre.

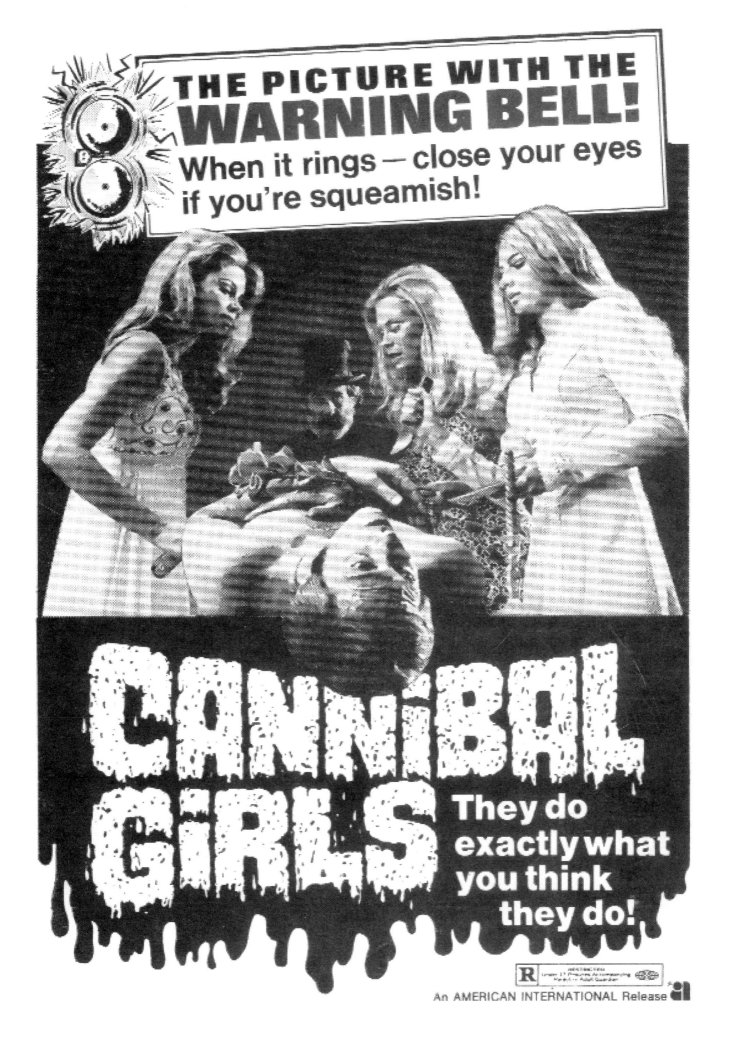

LEATHERFACE REDUX: THE SMALLER ECONOMY MODEL IN *Texas Chainsaw Massacre 2*.

HELL COMES TO YOUR HOUSE

The most truly frightening horrors are often found very close to home. Like the traffic statistic that reveals most automobile accidents occur within a finite radius of the driver's own domicile, one needn't venture very far to discover that terrible things can happen on very familiar ground. In horror films, the beasts that invade our sanctuaries are usually not from outer space, haunted graveyards or the netherworld. They can even be friends, lovers or complete strangers. Man is, and always will be, the most dangerous animal on the face of the earth.

Sometimes one's home may be a castle, laboratory or mausoleum as well. Since the beginnings of the horror film, really bad things have happened to those who believe they're safest at home. Perhaps confronting the reality that there are no real sanctuaries, no safe places whatsoever, is a deep-dish fear we all eventually, albeit reluctantly, must acknowledge. Most times we can keep the beasts at bay—by barricading ourselves behind sturdy walls, locking the doors and activating a security system. We cannot control these monsters, but the knowledge that they are somewhere out there, on the other side, can keep us from slipping into a deathly, crippling paranoid state.

When Walt Kelly, the venerable creator of the comic strip Pogo, announced within those panels that, "We have met the enemy—and he is us," a new, and very elusive, horror was called out of hiding. The theory of the 'beast within' has been a staple of religions, literature and the arts since time began. While many horror films have exploited this concept countless times, numerous mainstream films have also used this plot device to propel their stories and add a touch of malevolence to the commonplace.

Long before Sean Cunningham and Wes Craven bore witness to the atrocities committed in that *Last House on the Left (1972)*, other filmmakers

STRETCH AND CHOPTOP PLAY WITH FIRE IN *Texas Chainsaw Massacre 2*.

"YOU'RE NOT PUTTING *that* THING BETWEEN MY LEGS!" FOREPLAY *Texas Chainsaw Massacre 2*-STYLE.

THE FAMILY THAT SLAYS TOGETHER...STAYS TOGETHER.

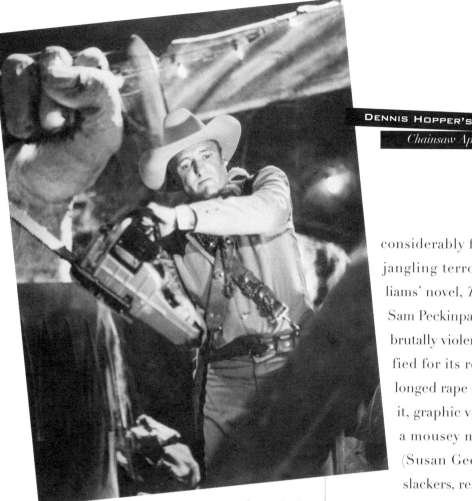

considerably for claustrophobic, nerve-jangling terror. Based on Gordon Williams' novel, *The Siege at Trencher's Farm*, Sam Peckinpah's highly controversial and brutally violent *Straw Dogs (1971)* was vilified for its realistic and painfully prolonged rape scenes, as well as its explicit, graphic violence. Dustin Hoffman is a mousey mathematician whose wife (Susan George) is assaulted by local slackers, resulting in a ferocious home invasion sequence that only Peckinpah would dare film. The film was cut by five minutes for its theatrical release and the full, unexpurgated director's cut hasn't been screened for over 3o years.

The theme has proved terribly resilient. Recent efforts like David Fincher's *Panic Room (2002)* and rocker Rob Zombie's *House of 1000 Corpses (2003)* prove there's still plenty of household horrors to go around.

Nearly every contemporary effort mining this fertile field, however, must be seen through the prism of *Last House on the Left*. This was the rare film, that despite the passage of time and the changing standards of explicit horrors, still retains its primeval power, reckless energy and its undeniable ability to shock you senseless.

Fledgling filmmakers Sean Cunningham and

explored the horror found at home. Nearly 2o years before Craven's film, several bold, fearless directors explored this territory with terrifying results.

William Wyler's *The Desperate Hours (1955)*, featuring an all-star cast including Humphrey Bogart, Frederic March, Arthur Kennedy and Gig Young, used Joseph Hayes' hair-raising novel (based on actual events) to terrific effect in this tense tale of escaped convicts terrorizing a suburban family. Robert Mitchum scorches the screen with unforgettably incendiary performances in both *Night of the Hunter (1955)* and *Cape Fear (1962)*, proving that man, indeed, could be the devil incarnate. Terence Young's *Wait Until Dark (1967)* with Audrey Hepburn as a blind woman attacked by thugs in her own apartment raised the bar

Wes Craven had been trying for years to break into the feature film arena, but their first collaborative effort was *Together*, a soft-core, pseudo-documentary about the swinging sex scene of the '70s. Marilyn Chambers (then Marilyn Biggs), who went on to porno super stardom with *Behind the Green Door (1972)*, made a brief appearance in one of the film's more controversial, explicit sex scenes. *Together* eventually returned a rather handsome profit and both Cunningham and Craven were ready to up the ante and further their mutual adventure in feature filmmaking. Decades later, the filmmakers agreed that their major motivations were to make a cheap film, show realistic, explicit violence, and further hone their craft.

Needless to say, the mission was accomplished and the low-budget, confrontational horror film would never, ever, be the same again. The filmmakers kept it cheap—real cheap. The original budget was only about $45,000 for a Super 16mm print; and even when it was blown up for 35mm theatrical showings, the budget stayed under $100,000. Principal photography began in the Fall of 1971 and the film was shot in and around Westport, Connecticut. However, it wasn't always planned as *Last House on the Left*. That title came almost by accident, the result of a casual, offhand remark. Other titles the filmmakers toyed with include: *Krug and Company*, *Sex Crime of the Century*, *Night of Vengeance* and *The Men's Room*.

Whatever the title it played under, it created a firestorm of frenzied interest—both pro and con. Most critics fired vicious and alarming salvos

R.A. MIHAILOFF ONCE AGAIN PROVES SIZE *does* MATTER IN *Leatherface: Texas Chainsaw Massacre 3*.

towards the filmmakers, citing the explicit violence, twisted sex, misogynistic excesses and hypocritical posturings. Oddly enough, noted film critic Roger Ebert was one of its staunchest supporters. He awarded the film three-and-a-half stars, calling it a "...tough, bitter little sleeper... sheer and unexpected terror...about four times as good as you'd expect." Even if most critics either loathed the film or dismissed it condescendingly, they simply could not ignore it. Hallmark Releasing Corp., famed for their exploitation promotional formula that catapulted the German-made *Mark of the Devil (1969)* to a box-office bonanza, created quite a buzz for *Last House* with their in-your-face campaign. When Hallmark acquired the rights to *Mark of the Devil*, they set to work on an advertising blitz that would burn that title into the brains of millions of drive-in sleazophiles. Calling it, "Positively...the Most Horrifying Film Ever Made" and "the first film rated 'V' for violence," the good folks at Hallmark also provided audiences with a way cool, illustrated souvenir that eventually became quite a collectible: the *Mark of the Devil* barf bag. For *Last House on the Left*, Hallmark asked "Can a movie go too far?" The distributors also suggested that to avoid fainting, "Keep repeating...it's only a movie...only a movie." That tag line was terribly effective, but definitely not the brainchild of Hallmark alone. Variations of the line were also used in campaigns for both William Castle's *Straight-Jacket (1964)* and Herschell Gordon Lewis' *Color Me Blood Red (1965)*.

The other catchy slogan, "Mari, 17, is dying... even for her the worst is yet to come,"set an edgy, morbid tone to the film, one which it truly lives up to. Even when the critics were going for the throat, the distributors answered with yet another ploy: a phony, bullshit disclaimer that accompanied the ad-mats in some major U.S. markets. Without one whiff of irony to cloud the senses, Hallmark insisted that the film was really, "a plea for an end to all the senseless violence and inhuman cruelty that has become so much a part of the times in which we live." Really! One might be tempted, then, to surmise that *The Texas Chainsaw Massacre (1974)* is really a veiled cry for "the safe and responsible use of power tools."

Regardless of the film's back story, its notorious cult reputation, or the provocative advertising campaign used to sell it, the most compelling question remains: Does it live up to the hype? And for once, a resounding, "Well, fuck yes!" The passing decades have not eroded its reputation whatsoever—it remains just as troubling, inflammatory, confrontational and gut-churning as ever. Thirty years later, MGM Studios released a bargain-priced DVD with what is probably the most definitive, full-length and "Unrated" version that we'll ever see. However, the added or enhanced footage does little, if anything, to embellish the ferocious power this nasty little film has always possessed.

Loosely based on Ingmar Bergman's Academy-Award winning *The Virgin Spring (1960)*, Cunningham and Craven's film maintains a parallel plot, but soon veers decidedly off-road and deep into classic exploitation territory. While Bergman's film is a Medieval Swedish fable about the rape and murder of a farmer's daughter by a roving gang of psycho shepherds, *Last House* is a very contemporary tale that could easily be

JIM SIEDOW (THE COOK) WONDERS IF THIS *Chainsaw* SEQUEL WILL SPILL THE BEANS ON THE FAMILY'S SECRET SAUCE.

"ripped from the headlines!" of any daily newspaper. There is no comfort taken in the myth, the fable, of the rape/murder/revenge scenario. Craven shoves it right in your face without apology and without adornment. There is no 'distancing' mechanism, no cinematic tomfoolery, to allow the audience any degree of relief. The horror is right there—in the same room, practically on top of you—threatening to engulf the viewer in its ugly maelstrom of hate, brutality and bloodshed.

The plotline is bareboned, cut to its essence. Two girls are kidnapped, sexually assaulted and murdered by a gang of psycho-perverts. By accident, the killers end up at the house of one of the murdered girls and are then viciously killed by the parents in a bloody, vengeful, and prolonged climax. In many ways, *Last House on the Left* unfolds like many other exploitation potboilers, but soon reveals its true intent: it's going to take you places you've never, ever been before. David Hess (who also composed and performed the musical score) is a seething, highly-combustible presence as 'Krug,' the de-facto leader of the gang of thugs, who is continually propelling the intensity of the violent confrontations to hair-raising levels. Audiences were not quite prepared for some of the more explicit scenes: a graphic disembowelment; sadistic torture; sexual humiliation and a castration-during-fellatio sequence that still hurts to this very day. Soon, the film was being referred to as the one that "launched a 1000 lunches." The newly-released, supposedly uncut print from MGM DVD restores much of the disembowelment scene as well as the sequence in which Krug carves his name into Mari's chest. Originally rated "X" by the MPAA (for obvious reasons), legend has it that Cunningham simply pasted the "R"-rating designation from another film onto the first reel of *Last House* and sent the print on its way. Neither Cunningham nor Craven have ever really agreed to the "hows and whys" of all the various cuts of the film released over the years, and neither has been able to successfully cobble together the definitive version The most complete version, released by MGM in 2002, was supplemented by footage supplied by the film's "unofficial archivist," filmmaker Roy (*Document of the Dead*) Frumkes, who had previously worked with Craven on the unreleased anthology film *Tales That'll Tear Your Heart Out*.

Last House on the Left was part of a swarm of new, angry and intensely confrontational horror films that seemed to try and address some of the troubling aspects of a convulsing, roiling American landscape desperately recoiling from years of war, racism, political assassinations, government scandals, riots and rampage. As the very fabric of Americana was being stretched, torn and sometimes shredded, many filmmakers seized the opportunity to confront the audience with controversial scenes and topics that seemed to mirror some of the real horrors seen nightly during the TV news broadcasts. Wes Craven has drawn parallels to the Vietnam War, with its daily body counts and televised atrocities, to the hostile foreboding landscape he tried to create in *Last House on the Left*. American society—in the wake of Vietnam, Watergate, the Kennedy-King assassina-

THE ORIGINAL
LEATHERFACE
(GUNNAR HANSEN)
ENJOYING A MOMENT
OF PRE-MEATHOOK
MAYHEM.

tions, escalating racial tensions, police riots and Charles Manson—was clearly in a troubling, transformational stage. Mainstream cinema took up the challenge as well; many critics see this period as one of the most expressive and challenging eras in cinema history. Films like *Bonnie and Clyde (1967)*, *The Wild Bunch (1969)*, *The Godfather (1972)*, *The Conversation (1974)*, *Chinatown (1974)*, *Dog Day Afternoon (1975)*, *Taxi Driver (1976)*, *The Deer Hunter (1978)* and *Apocalypse Now (1979)* tackled some hefty issues and dramatically raised the stakes for a new breed of renegade filmmakers. For horror films, the traditional "boogeyman" was being supplanted by the madman lurking just next door.

Tobe Hooper, whose short documentaries and sole feature film, *Eggshells (1970)*, had earned him somewhat of a local reputation, was aching to break out from the college film school scene, especially after catching a 16mm screening of George Romero's *Night of the Living Dead* during a University film festival. His artsy-fartsy, hippie dippy *Eggshells*, about the disintegration of a commune and the end of the "Love Generation," was well received and won an award at the Atlanta Film Festival. His next film would forever change the landscape of modern horror, in much the same way as Alfred Hitchcock's *Psycho (1960)* did nearly a decade and a half before. Plundering much the same source material appropriated by Hitchcock in his research for *Psycho*, Hooper also returned to the curious story of Edward C. Gein. A part-time babysitter and handyman, Gein was also a full-time Mama's boy and, later, a murderer, grave robber, cannibal and sexual freakazoid. Taken to wearing the flayed skin of his mother,

strapping on a scalped, spray-painted set of female genitalia and howling at the moon, Gein was caught in a house filled with human skin and bones, nipple belts, internal organs and a naked and flayed body, dressed out like a deer, hanging upside down in his workshop. Necrophilia was also suspected. Gein was also the "inspiration" for *Deranged (1972)*, starring Roberts Blossom as "Ezra Cobb, the Butcher of Woodside."

Filming began on *The Texas Chainsaw Massacre* in July, 1973, at an isolated farmhouse on Quick Hill Road, just outside the dinky burg of Round Rock. Hooper and co-creator Kim Henkel formed Vortex pictures and shot the film in 16mm for around $140,000. Later, actor Gunnar (Leatherface) Hansen would quip to your reporter in casual conversation that they "could've done it for half that" if they really knew what they were doing. Principal photography was completed in 32 days during a scorching summer that turned the set, adorned with real animal skins and remains, into a sweltering charnel house. Since much of the famed "dinner table sequence" had to be filmed at night, the windows were draped shut and the stench from the rotting carcasses soon became the stuff of legend.

On its way to becoming a contemporary horror classic, Hooper's seminal film also managed to effectively de-construct the All American Nuclear Family Unit, replacing it with a murderous clan of dysfunctional, grave-robbing cannibals who preyed on the lost, helpless and infirm. Hooper's dystopian view of family life was extrapolated into his decidedly twisted take on yet another American institution—The Road Trip. Usually a liberating journey of discovery and renewal,

Hooper's route was strictly a Road to Ruin. His hapless travelers, expecting perhaps some degree of sympathy and assistance on their wayward plight, are instead confronted with the Slaughterhouse Sledgehammer Logic of the imposing Leatherface, a towering, man-mountain meateater clearly at the top of the back road's food chain. Hooper also toyed a bit with our traditional view on movie heroes—much like Romero did with the unlikely black sole survivor in *Night of the Living Dead*—by killing off everyone but the plucky Sally (Marilyn Burns) by the film's frenzied climax. Besides being a resourceful, highly resilient and never-say-die kind of gal, Burns had some World Class pipes and a full-throttled scream that could shatter glass at 300 paces. Nobody, but nobody, screams like that anymore. Perhaps Hooper was also being a bit prescient in his choice of a New Age heroine, ushering in a new distaff sensibility echoed in numerous films that followed. Just consider who's left standing at the end of *Halloween* (1978), *I Spit on Your Grave* (1978), *Alien* (1979) and *A Nightmare on Elm Street* (1982).

And, despite the film's notorious reputation and its sublimely arresting title, *The Texas Chainsaw Massacre* remains a relatively bloodless film. Younger fans weaned on such graphic fare as *Dawn of the Dead* (1979), *Friday the 13th* (1980) or *The Evil Dead* (1982), are usually nonplussed at the lack of sanguinary spillage in a film with such a slimy, suggestive title. Although the theatrical poster screamed, "Who will survive...and what will be left of them?", the film is relatively restrained, polite even, by today's standards.

Hooper's film was truly an instance of lightning being caught in a bottle, because the subse-quent sequels, including Hooper's own *The Texas Chainsaw Massacre 2* (1986), would never again come close to capturing the mayhem, menace and indeed, magic, of the original. Jeff Burr's *Leatherface (1990)* was a solid, journeyman effort, but both his film and Kim Henkel's *Texas Chainsaw Massacre: The Next Generation (1996)*, did little, if anything, to further The Mythos of the Saw. Burr was handicapped by nosey studio suits, was subsequently fired, and replaced by a director who shot a lame, totally illogical ending to replace Burr's fiercely nihilistic one. Kim Henkel's version is nearly a flat-out, xerox copy of the original whose main distinction seems to be his introduction of fledgling superstars Renee (*Jerry Maguire, Chicago*) Zellweger and Matthew (*Amistad, How to Lose a Guy in 10 Days*) McConaughey. Henkel also deserves a whack upside the head with a sledgehammer for his scurrilously effeminate portrayal of the new Leatherface character. A real boneheaded bit of casting there, and an unconscionable disgrace to Gunnar Hansen's definitive performance.

The Texas Chainsaw Massacre has aged quite well; and despite three decades worth of competition, it remains—as one wit so aptly stated—"The *Gone With the Wind* of Meat Movies." The film has also found a home with the Museum of Modern Art in New York City, as part of their permanent collection. And, the less said about the threatened remake by Michael (*Pearl Harbor*) Bay, the better.

Meir Zarchi's troubling and highly controversial *I Spit on Your Grave (1978)* fanned the flames of

No one, but *no* one screams like Marilyn Burns.

critical derision, finding few, if any, allies. Roger Ebert, effusive in his praise of *Last House on the Left*, spat out this review: "A vile bag of garbage... for vicious sex criminals. Sick, reprehensible and contemptible." Even John Waters, whose films like *Mondo Trasho (1969)*, *Pink Flamingos (1972)* and *Female Trouble (1974)* were often described in similar terms, called the film: "Impossible to defend. The vice squad ought to watch every person who actually buys this film. It even managed to offend me." Another brutal critical salvo named *I Spit on Your Grave* as "the most reprehensible film ever made. Anyone who defends it must be hopelessly perverted." Whoaa there, now, pardner.

With frothing, hypertensive reviews like that, it's little wonder that the film was released under the appropriate banner of "Jerry Gross presents..." This, of course, is the same drive-in slime czar who brought you *Africa: Blood and Guts (1970)* and those "Two Great Blood-Horrors to Rip Out Your Guts!": *I Drink Your Blood (1971)* and *I Eat Your Skin (1964)*. When Zarchi's film was released under its original title, *Day of the Woman*, nobody gave a shit. By nicking the name of an obscure, French film made in 1964, and unveiling a new, racy poster design, the Jerry Gross gang bragged that their brand new "*Woman*" had just "...cut, chopped, broken and burned five men beyond recognition...But no jury in America would ever convict her!" No matter there were only four; and even after repeat viewings, most will miss both the "broken" and "burned" dude too. The U.S. poster also featured a barely clothed, bloodied actress, bearing absolutely no resemblance whatsoever to star Camille Keaton (yes, she of the famous Buster K. family), clutching a huge knife

by its blade. The tagline promised "An Act of Revenge!" Oh, they were right about that, yes indeed.

Director Zarchi, a filmmaker with dubious credentials, relished the critical firestorm the re-release ignited. "It was good for me, good publicity; it sells more movie tickets and it brought the film to the attention of a lot of people." Zarchi claimed he based the film on a real-life incident in which he and a companion rescued a girl who had been robbed, beaten and raped by two men in a park. After wrapping the naked, hysterical woman (who also reportedly suffered a broken jaw) in a coat and accompanying her to the nearest police station, Zarchi was aghast at the callous indifference and accusatory tone of the officers taking her report. "What were you doing in the park? Should we notify your mother?" Zarchi noted the police were far more concerned about completing their paperwork than in providing comfort for the victim or even in apprehending her assailants. In Zarchi's film, the raped and savagely beaten heroine goes after her attackers by herself—and kills all of them. When one of the rapists has his manhood removed during an impromptu bit of home surgery, Zarchi doesn't flinch. He never portrays her actions as anything less than triumphant. The film ends with a freeze frame: the woman, axe in hand and thrust overhead in victory, speeds away in a motor boat, a slight smile beginning to crease her face. And unlike the phony moral posturings of *Last House on the Left*, which attempts to posit the notion that all violence is ultimately demeaning and vulgar for all involved, Zarchi's film avoids judgement and just lets the action play itself out. The heroine simply gets away with it, and she's not likely to ever get caught either. And, judging by the last image seen on screen, she appears to be neither demeaned nor devastated by what she's done.

Zarchi toyed with this potent exploitation formula once again with *Don't Mess with My Sister!* *(1989)*, but toned down the vicious and explicit elements considerably. The film stands as a wimpy, gutless, routine potboiler that might have safely played on the Disney Channel during prime time.

Though both *I Spit on Your Grave* and *The Texas Chainsaw Massacre* established motifs that were aped repeatedly for decades, it was *Last House on the Left* that launched a flurry of films dealing with the house and home and the horrors within. Houses sprang up all over the world where, sometimes, the Gateway to Hell was often as close as the front door.

Though Italian maestro Mario Bava's *Twitch of the Death Nerve (1972)* (aka *Bay of Blood*, *Carnage*) had nothing whatsoever in common with Craven's film, it was released in many markets as *Last House on the Left II*, accompanied by a deceptive ad campaign designed to downplay its foreign origins and ignore its totally dissimilar plotline. Bava's film is actually a highly accomplished, sardonic proto-stalk 'n' slasher that predated *Friday the 13th* by nearly a decade in its inventive use of the "creative kill" and the ever-escalating body count.

Roger Watkin's unfinished 1972 student film, originally titled *The Funhouse* and *Cuckoo Clocks of Hell*, was re-cut and retitled by clueless distributors and released with yet another disingenuous and misleading ad campaign as *Last House on Dead End Street (1977)*. Though an abandoned col-

lege building stands in for the titular house of the title, the brutality, bloodshed and sheer madness seen here would manage to raise the bar considerably in terms of on-screen debauchery. In one lengthy and excruciatingly protracted sequence (severely trimmed in most release prints), a woman is tied down upon an ersatz operating table and slowly dismembered, piece by bloody piece. She is revived again and again by smelling salts, only to be summarily gutted by tin snips; her glistening viscera passed around the room by a gang of snickering miscreants attempting to produce a real "snuff" film. Though another character has his eyeball punctured by a power drill in tender, loving closeup, the most deranged sequence remains the justifiably infamous "Deer's Foot Blowjob Scene." Uh...let me explain. As one blubbering lobster is forced to kneel, a topless skank inserts a severed deer's hoof in her zipper and forces the dude to fellate the foot. Standing behind her is another freak holding two more deer's feet over her head like satanic horns. The scene must be seen to be believed.

Released as both *Last House on the Left II* and *The New House on the Left*, Aldo Lado's *The Night Train Murders (1974)* stays closest to the tone and plottings of Craven's film, merely substituting (yeh, you guessed it) a moving train as the setting for the ensuing debauchery. Margaret and Lisa are two school chums returning home to Italy to spend the Christmas holidays with Lisa's parents. When a gang of degenerates climbs aboard their train, the girls are beaten, raped and killed. Both bodies are then tossed from the moving train. However, waiting patiently at the station to pick up the girls are Lisa's parents—who've obviously

"★★★ ½ ...SHEER AND UNEXPECTED TERROR!
A TOUGH, BITTER LITTLE SLEEPER OF A
MOVIE ABOUT FOUR TIMES AS GOOD AS YOU'D
EXPECT! UNBEARABLE TENSION!" – Chicago Sun Times

MARI,
SEVENTEEN, IS
DYING. EVEN FOR
HER THE WORST
IS YET
TO
COME!

TO AVOID
FAINTING
KEEP REPEATING,
IT'S ONLY A MOVIE
..ONLY A MOVIE
..ONLY A MOVIE
..ONLY A MOVIE
..ONLY A MOVIE
ONLY A MOVIE

...IT'S JUST
ACROSS THE
STREET FROM
"JOE"!

WARNING!
NOT RECOMMENDED
FOR PERSONS
OVER 30!

LAST HOUSE ON THE LEFT

SEAN S. CUNNINGHAM FILMS LTD. Presents "THE LAST HOUSE
ON THE LEFT" Starring DAVID HESS • LUCY GRANTHAM •
SANDRA CASSEL • MARC SHEFFLER • and introducing
ADA WASHINGTON • Produced by SEAN S. CUNNINGHAM
Written and Directed by WES CRAVEN • COLOR BY MOVIELAB

R RESTRICTED Under 17 requires
accompanying Parent or Adult Guardian

- THEATRE IMPRINT -

already seen Craven's film — and know precisely what's expected of them. Prolific composer Ennio Morricone provided most of the film's haunting and highly effective musical score.

House by the Lake (1976) (aka *Death Weekend*) stars the raspy-voiced Brenda Vaccaro as a model boffing a self-absorbed, weasely dentist (aren't they all?) at his private lakeside manor. Due to a previous error in judgement showcasing an appalling disregard for highway etiquette, Vaccaro and her spineless lover incur the wrath of a gang of sleazeballs led by a huffing, menacing Don Stroud. During an attempted rape, one creepazoid is again caught on the receiving end of a bit of improvised home surgery, losing his schlong to an expertly-wielded shard of glass. Though Vaccaro croaks her way through every scene, everybody dies at the end except our foghorn-throated heroine.

The rarely-seen and obviously re-titled oddity *The Last House on the Beach (1977)* was an Italian cheapie directed by Franco (*Mondo Cane, The Wild Beasts*) Prosperi, in which a gang of bankrobbers lay siege on an isolated beach house; this time conveniently occupied by a group of Catholic schoolgirls and their teacher, a nun. The sexual assaults, including the nun's rape and an extended, slow-motion penetration by a huge wooden staff, prove far more potent and disturbing than the various methods of mayhem used to dispatch the attackers during the film's violent final reel.

Wes Craven returned home again with *Stranger in Our House (1978)* (aka *Summer of Fear*), a tepid TV thriller starring Linda (*The Exorcist*) Blair in a battle of wits with a hillbilly witch. Craven would continue his explorations of the horrors of both home and family through several other features including *The Hills Have Eyes (1977)*, *A Nightmare on Elm Street (1984)* and *The People Under the Stairs (1991)*.

After scaring the living shit out of folks in *Last House on the Left*, maniac-for-hire David Hess was the Devil in a Winnebago opposite Franco Nero in the sleazy ('natch) psycho road pic, *Hitch Hike (1978)*, before returning to the familiar trappings of Ruggero (*Cannibal Holocaust*) Deodato's *House on the Edge of the Park (1980)*. Again, Hess plays a raping, murderous thug tormenting a trendy group of bored yuppies who've just made the mistake of their snotty little lives by deciding to party with him and his 'tardo sidekick (John Morghen). Seeing Hess wielding a very menacing straight razor while maintaining a nearly nonstop barrage of abusive chatter remains chillingly effective, though Deodato nearly blows it all by a flaccid, anti-climactic ending that robs the film of much of its perverse power.

Any film that is bookended by alarming scenes of child abuse, rife with misogynistic venom and relentless in its depictions of lingering torture, is bound to win few fans and even fewer critics. Joseph Ellison's creepy and perverse *Don't Go in the House (1980)* follows the career trajectory of an abused, nerdish mama's boy, who lures young bimbos into his home-based, steel-paneled crematorium and burns them alive with a flame-thrower. It's slickly produced and efficiently made, but the film's risible moral tone; scurrilous dialog; and overtly sadistic trappings make it a real tough sell. The truly hair-raising, mightily disturbing burn makeups by Tom Brumberger are all too real, as is the film's conceit that child abuse is a hopeless, never-ending cycle passed from one generation to the next.

The stupid and infantile *Horror House on Highway Five (1985)* features a gang of sub-par maniacs-in-training—one addled by brain parasites and another in a cheapjack Richard Nixon Halloween mask—trying vainly to generate some commotion among a group of dim-bulb, party-hearty college twits. Frequently punctuated by insufferably bad rock tunes performed by a band of tone deaf microcephalics, this loser belongs in a ditch alongside the real Highway to Hell.

Michael Haneke's *Funny Games (1997)* wants oh-so desperately to be a German version of *Last House on the Edge of a Lakeside Park*, but its dime-store maniacs haven't the wattage to even fire up a bedside night light. Despite several flirtations with moments of a vile and vicious nature (including an unwelcome striptease by a leathery, butt-ugly Kraut hag) this surly yakfest thinks it's about ten times more clever and frightening than it actually is. The posturing film school brats behind this lifeless dreck would surely wet themselves and cry for their mommies if David Hess were to appear and merely ask them for the time of day. Even the tortured bleatings of some hamsters on crack masquerading as a punk band fail to add any spice to this soggy soufflé.

Even as we slip slowly into the new millennium, filmmakers have yet to exhaust all the possibilities of this rather narrow, microcosmic sub-genre, and continue to explore, exploit and re-invent scenarios that keep the horrors homeward bound. The formula may be deceptively simple and unadorned, but the effect of juxtaposing chaos, terror and ultraviolence within the context of supposedly safe environment remains chillingly effective.

David (*Seven*) Fincher's *Panic Room (2002)* keeps the horror and suspense tightly shuttered and claustrophobically focused by sequestering star Jodie Foster and her wimpy daughter in a steel reinforced "safe room" for most of the film (it was originally going to be a one-set feature) as a motley crew of robbers search for a hidden fortune. And guess where that money is actually stashed? Oh, there now, I've gone and spoiled it for you. Led by the usually affable Forrest Whitaker, the gang also includes country crooner Dwight Yoakum, whose really scary pate should really be addressed by a studio directive requiring a hat at all times. Though not nearly as tense and nerve-jangling as one might expect from the director of the lacerating *Seven*, Fincher keeps the film inside the house and the "safe room" for most of the running time, rarely venturing outside, and maintains a tight lid on the simmering, escalating tensions between predator and prey.

Heavy metal rocker Rob Zombie, a lifelong horror fan, has always been forthright about his contempt for the contemporary horror film, frequently venting his spleen by openly admitting, "I want to like the new stuff, but it's always crap. It seems as if anything made after 1985 is hopeless." His assessment of the *Scream* trilogy is unsparing: "I hate that shit with a passion. It's a bunch of teeny-bopper crap meant to sell more tacos at Taco Bell." He concludes with a weary sigh, "Nothing seems scary anymore." Thankfully then, in his directorial feature film debut, Zombie gets back to the basics, revisiting *Texas Chainsaw Massacre* territory with a loving and respectful vengeance. Early screenings of *House of 1000 Corpses (2003)* attended by Universal Studios suits were met with abject shock and revulsion. "It's far more intense than anything we had come to expect," they bleated. What? An intense, troubling horror flick? The fuckin' shame! Universal pissed their collective pants, cut the film loose and suggested Zombie take his little film out behind the barn and shoot it. Lions Gate Releasing eventually picked it up and blurted,

"We're gonna have some fun with this campaign." With *House of 1000 Corpses*, Zombie has returned to the simple, primitive and in-your-face formula that has propelled his favorite (and ours as well) horror films of the '70s and early '80s. Because Zombie knows that when you approach a strange house occupied by even stranger people, you should expect no mercy. He knows full well that sometimes, when you call for help — you get hell instead.

ROBERT ENGLUND'S FREDDY KRUEGER, MASTER MILLENNIAL MADMAN.

EYES WIDE OPEN IN DARIO ARGENTO'S MASTERPIECE, *Opera*.

PASTALAND SPLATTER

Another major beneficiary of the '80s Video Revolution was the Italian horror film industry. Although numerous Italian productions were often seen in American theatres; they were usually atrociously dubbed, badly edited, retitled, scratchy prints that were second-billed to fourth-rate U.S. detritus.

Although Dario Argento's seminal *Suspiria* *(1976)* briefly played in American theatres ("the only thing more terrifying than the last 10 minutes...are the first 90"), it was the heavily cut version, minus major coverage of the film's first ghastly murders. That was usually the case with other foreign director's films as well. Most Italian titles were shorn of explicit shots of both sex and violence and frequently reedited into versions supposedly "more comprehensible" to U.S. audiences.

When the horror boom really began to erupt in the early '80s and the demand rapidly exceeded the theatrical supply, the videocassette re-corder played a pivotal role in giving the fans nearly anything they desired. When Japanese laser discs were introduced, many classic Italian horror films were released in their full-length, original form: uncut, unedited and often restored to their theatrical aspect ratio (letterboxed). Although it took over 12 years for Argento's *Suspiria* to be legitimately released in the States as a director's cut, it had been available for years in its original, unexpurgated version on Japanese laser disc. Fortunately, nearly all Argento's earlier works, including *Bird with the Crystal Plumage (1970)*, *Cat O' Nine Tails (1971)*, *Four Flies on Grey Velvet (1971)* and *Profondo Rosso (1975)* *(Deep Red)* have been made available through various foreign sources in the past in uncut form. Some of the most severe damage had been inflicted especially on Argento: *Deep Red* was severely trimmed and subtitled *Hatchet Murders* in the U.S.; *Tenebrae (1982)* lost 13 minutes and numerous gore scenes when it became *Unsane*; *Phenomena (1985)* was cut by over 20 minutes during its metamorphosis into *Creepers*. Only *Inferno (1980)*, in a limited release by Key Video, was preserved from Stateside tampering. Even Argento's most recent efforts have suffered in the hands of indifferent distributors. His modern giallo masterpiece *Opera (1987)* was poorly received in his native land and subsequently reedited into numerous variations. Even the Japanese laser disc release of *Terror at the Opera* ends arbitrarily, completely deleting Argento's controversial, but obviously heartfelt, coda. Fortunately, with the advent of the DVD format, the director's cut has been restored.

His most widely-seen theatrical film in the U.S. remains the unfortunate *Two Evil Eyes (1989)*, a mismatched directorial tribute to Edgar Allan Poe with George A. Romero. While Romero presents a predictable, somnambulant version of "Facts in the Case of M. Valdemar," Argento's reworking of "The Black Cat" shows brief, inspired glimpses of genius, seemingly misplaced in this oft-told tale. The opening sequence, though, shows Argento in all his gutsy glory. As an arthouse photographer (Harvey Keitel) records a grisly murder scene, a huge pendulum blade swings menacingly past him and through a neatly bisected, nude female body. It is pure, vintage Argento.

Because Argento so enjoyed working in the U.S., he returned to shoot *Aura's Enigma*, which featured his daughter Asia in the lead role. Lensed in Minneapolis and retitled *Trauma (1993)*, the film again featured the makeup FX by Tom Savini, whom Argento had previously worked with on both *Dawn of the Dead* and *Two Evil Eyes*. Asia Argento plays an anorexic, suicidal teen who

had witnessed the brutal decapitation of her parents by a psycho-killer dubbed the Headhunter. Despite several typically inspired sequences and signature set pieces, the film never really coalesces into much more than a warmed-up souffle of Argento's favorite recipe.

Shot in English and starring a name brand cast including Piper (*Carrie*) Laurie, Frederic Forest, Brad Dourif and James Russo, *Trauma* failed to ignite any critical acclaim (even among Argentophile genre pundits) and was given a low profile U.S. video release (in both "R" version and uncut) after a less-than-spectacular box office showing in Italy. The jury was split on the thespian abilities of daughter Asia, though, but ol' dad held even grander plans.

In *The Stendhal Syndrome (1996)*, Asia stars as a policewoman showing signs of the titular malady when she's overcome and collapses in front of a painting at the Uffizi Gallery. She dreams of sex with a humanoid sea bass and sees 3-D demon boners jutting out from graffitied walls. And, in tried and true Argento fashion, she begins forming some manner of psychic bond with a serial killer terrorizing Rome. Besides the cleverly orchestrated, stylized violence (special kudos to the slo-mo-bullet-through-the-cheek scene), there is a very ugly, protracted razor blade rape scene that provides troubling punctuation to this rather uncomfortable father/daughter scenario.

Even diehard Argentophiles couldn't make much of a case for the woebegotten *The Phantom of the Opera (1998)*, again inexplicably starring Asia Argento. She's a promising (oh, har har) young opera diva-to-be stalked by a lovelorn Julian (*Warlock*) Sands in full rock star mode. Since he

THE SHOCKING MURDERS THAT BEGIN ARGENTO'S *Suspiria*
WERE SEVERELY CUT IN MOST PRINTS.

MOST ARGENTOPHILES CONSIDER *Deep Red* THE MAESTRO'S FINEST HOUR.

was raised by a caring, nurturing community of rats, this "phantom" comes saddled with some serious identity issues. Argento had continually threatened to make this film for years, and once delivered, a solid case for a pre-emptive, third term cinematic abortion was successfully made.

Argento finally dumped his daughter (who later co-starred with Vin Deisel in *XXX*) and made a half-hearted return to his giallo roots with *I Can't Sleep (2000)* (aka *Nonhosonno, Sleepless*). The great Max Von Sydow is wasted as a retired detective drawn into a series of murders that bear an uncanny resemblance to an old, closed case he once solved. Too bad it was the infamous "Dwarf Killer File" we're forced to revisit, as Argento spins his wheels trying to make a height-challenged miscreant even remotely menacing. It's a fragmented, illogical narrative (never Argento's

strong suit anyway), frequently interrupted by scenes that seem lifted directly from previous features. Perhaps their inclusion is Argento's way of paying a long overdue homage to himself, but it simply reminds us that we've been here before. Not that an "Argento's Greatest Hits" package wouldn't be welcomed, but *I Can't Sleep* seems curiously anemic, casting further doubt on the future of the venerable Italian maestro.

Argento has always remained one of the busiest auteurs, either on his own theatrical and television projects, or those of his hand-picked acolytes: Lamberto Bava and Michele Soavi. Argento co-wrote and produced Bava's rollicking *Demons (1985)* and its tacky sequel *Demons 2: The Nightmare Returns (1987)*. He performed similarly for Michele Soavi with *The Church (1989)* and *The Sect (1991)* (aka *The Devil's Daughter*). And,

Opera WAS A MASTERPIECE, REGARDLESS OF WHICH VERSION YOU SAW.

ARGENTO'S *Trauma* FEATURED DAUGHTER ASIA, SEVERAL MISPLACED NOGGINS AND A COOL PORTABLE GUILLOTINE.

when Lucio Fulci died unexpectedly during pre-production, Argento went on to produce Sergio Stivaletti's directorial debut, *The Wax Mask (1997)*. Argento is also the subject of Michele Soavi's superlative and mesmerizing documentary, *The Horror World of Dario Argento (1987)* as well as Luigi Cozzi's ersatz "sequel," *Dario Argento: Master of Horror (1993)*. Despite an uneven and oft-times wildly imbalanced career, Argento remains a towering genre presence: a passionate, dedicated and restless artiste; a tireless visionary; and a man very much in love with his work.

When Lucio Fulci died suddenly in March, 1996, the World of Horror lost one its most beloved filmmakers. (For more Fulci filmography, see both "Zombies" and "Chunkblowers.") From a professional career dating back to 1959, Fulci produced an amazingly prodigious body of work,

criss-crossing through every genre imaginable. Though Fulci came to U.S. gorehounds' attention through his ferocious zombie chunkblowers of the '80s, he dabbled in Westerns (*Four of the Apocalypse [1975]*), rock & roll comedies (*Juke Box Boys [1959]*), supernatural thrillers (*A Lizard in a Woman's Skin [1971]* , *The Psychic [1977]*), gangster flicks (*Contraband [1980]*), sci-fi potboilers (*Fighter Centurions [1983]*), and children's films (*White Fang [1973]*). Fulci died just as a career renaissance was slowly taking shape, so the directorial chores in his "comeback" film, the Argento-produced *The Wax Mask (1997)* went instead to FX specialist Sergio Stivaletti.

Fulci was much beloved by fans worldwide who flocked to various conventions in the '90s that began paying tribute to the Maestro and his films. His most ardent supporters felt Fulci never

LAMBERTO BAVA'S *Demons*:

HARD ROCK SPLATTER.

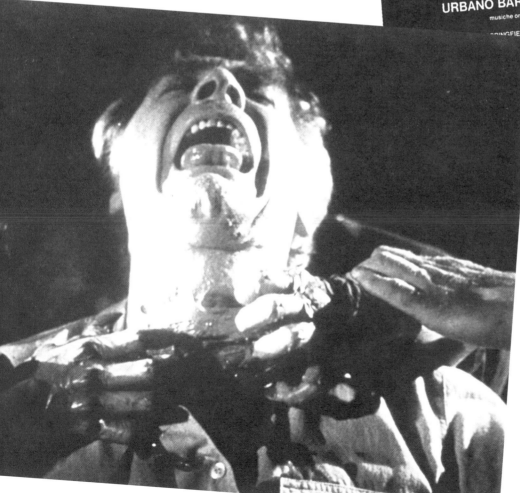

.... faranno dei cimiteri le loro cattedrali
e delle città le vostre tombe.

DARIO ARGENTO
presenta

DĒMONI

un film di LAMBERTO BAVA
URBANO BARBERINI · NATASHA HOVEY
musiche originali di CLAUDIO SIMONETTI

brani originali di:
PRINGFIELD · MOTLEY CRUE · SCORPIONS · GO WEST
RES · BILLY IDOL · ACCEPT · SAXON
RIO ARGENTO per la DACFILM   DOLBY STEREO

ARGENTO'S *Inferno* WAS ONE OF THE FEW FILMS RELEASED UNCUT IN THE U.S.

received enough credit for his work, seemingly always eclipsed by the towering shadow cast by fellow countryman Dario Argento. When two New York filmmakers made *Lucio Fulci: Maestro of Horror*, a loving tribute that often screened before Fulci's festival appearances, many felt that his Time Had Truly Come. Sadly, it did; but instead of triumph, there were tears instead. "Fulci was much more of an innovator than most people thought. He was pre-Argento," said Howard Berger, one of the filmmakers. During his festival appearances preceding his untimely death, Fulci was finally given the degree of respect and admiration that had so cruelly eluded him throughout much of his career. "Here was a genius," added Berger. "It was if Hitchcock were in the same room." Rest in Peace, Maestro.

Lamberto Bava, after serving a well-documented apprenticeship both with his father Mario and other Italian directors (he was Ruggero Deodato's assistant on *Cannibal Holocaust*), directed *Macabro (1980)* (aka *Frozen Terror*) as his feature film debut. The definitive severed noggin-in-a-fridge thriller, *Macabro* is a tightly constructed, bizarre character study with a deliciously twisted payoff.

La Casa con la Scala nel buio (1983) (aka *A Blade in the Dark*) is a full-throttle giallo with more than a nod to the style of Argento. When a composer retires to a huge, isolated villa to prepare the score for an upcoming suspense thriller, a series of mysterious assaults seem to be reflective of similar scenes in the movie-in-progress. Bava pays slavish homage to Argento in a scene deeply reminiscent of the famous

teeth-bashing sequence found in *Deep Red*. When a woman is cornered by the killer, her hand is knifed to a cabinet before she's suffocated with a plastic bag. She's then whacked repeatedly against the sink before her throat is slit. Michele Soavi was Bava's assistant director as well, playing the transvestite killer revealed during the film's climax.

Bava strayed from the parameters of the giallo film with the soft-core, titty follies of *Le Foto de Gloia (1983)* and the lame *Rambo* and *Jaws* knock-offs, *Blastfighter (1984)* and *Rosso Nell Oceano (1984)* (aka *Devouring Waves, Monster Fish*). Teaming with Argento, Bava's *Demons (1986)* became a huge box office hit in Italy and one of the most enthusiastically reviewed genre titles of the year. The sequel was woefully anemic, featuring an unwanted plethora of lousy, *Ghoulies*-style hand puppets jumping out of television screens and into the faces of dozens of wastrels in a high rise apartment building.

Bereft of the tuteledge of Argento, Bava tackled a number of corny television projects including *Dentro al Cimitero* (aka *Graveyard Disturbance*) *(1986)* and *The Ogre (1987)* which were met with a flurry of critical scorn. The release of *La Maschera del Demonio (1988)* (aka *The Devil's Veil*), was a well-executed, updated homage to his father's masterwork *Black Sunday (1960)*. Bava's later *Body Puzzle (1992)* also showed he had shed the spectre of Argento and found his own focus.

Michele Soavi also appeared as an actor in *La Maschera del Demonio* and his genre credits are nearly as pedigreed as Bava's. Besides directing *The Horror World of Dario Argento*, Soavi was the horrified boyfriend of the puking girl in Fulci's

Gates of Hell; the masked ticket handler in *Demons* and Argento's assistant on *Tenebrae* and *Phenomena*. He also served Terry Gilliam as an assistant director on the ill-fated, grotesquely over-budgeted *The Adventures of Baron Munchausen (1989)*.

Soavi's feature film directorial debut was the razor-sharp, tightly-plotted, masked killer thriller *Stagefright (1987)* (aka *Aquarius*, *Deliria*). Produced by Aristide Massacessi (Joe D'Amato) from a story by long-time crony Luigi Montefiore (aka George Eastman, the *Grim Reaper* hisself), *Stagefright* is a directorial tour-de-force, firmly

The Church is a confident, classy supernatural thriller boasting fluid and expressive cinematography (very reminiscent of prime Argento); haunting *mise-en-scenes*; generous doses of both creatures and carnage (by Sergio Stivaletti); and a pounding yet elegant score by Keith Emerson, Simon Boswell, Phillip Glass and Goblins.

Argento again produced and co-wrote Soavi's third feature, *The Devil's Daughter (1991)* (filmed as *The Sect*), about a cult that picks Kelly Curtis (Jamie Lee's sister) as the mother of the anti-Christ. The script is inventive and compelling,

and undisputably establishing Soavi as heir apparent to the throne of Argento.

Seeking to complete a *Demons* trilogy, Argento had toyed with the idea of *Demon Cathedral* as the series coda, before *The Church (1989)* (*La Chiesa*) came to fruition with Michele Soavi again at the helm. Co-written and co-produced by Argento,

yet wildly uneven. Scenes involving a crafty rabbit operating a TV remote control; the attack of a killer pelican; and the continuous misquoting of a key line from the Rolling Stones' "Sympathy for the Devil" are unnecessary distractions from the film's preachy, but deadly serious tone.

Soavi made nearly everyone a True Believer

ABOVE: THE DEVIL AND MISS JONES: BARE-ASSED AND BLASPHEMOUS IN *The Church*.

LEFT: DEVILISH DOINGS IN MICHELE SOAVI'S *The Church*.

PAGES 52-53: THE MEDIEVAL MASSACRE SCENE FROM *The Church*.

TISA FARROW AND THE AUTO-CANNIBALIZING *Anthropophagus* BEAST.

once again with the self-assured panache of *Dellamorte, Dellamore (1994)*, a wickedly surreal and grimly humorous tale of a cemetery caretaker's ongoing battles with the living dead. Called "returners" in the film, these zombies are a sometimes frisky, resourceful and libidinous lot, managing to teach both Dellamore (Rupert Everett) and his near-mute assistant Gnaghi (Francois Hadji-Lazaru) a thing or two about the sex lives of the recently deceased. Soavi's brilliant, eclectic direction; Everett's nicely modulated, compassionate performance (and an endearing one by Hadji-Lazaru); and Sergio Stivaletti's best make-ups to date add up to one fine, truly sublime, Thinking Man's Zombie Film.

Director Martin Scorsese was an early support-er of Soavi's, and no doubt helped in acquiring a Stateside distributor, thereby avoiding the usual direct-to-video fate bestowed upon most Italian genre offerings. October Films, who had previously released the much acclaimed nouveau vampire flick *Cronos (1994)* and two black- and-white, arthouse bloodsuckers, *Nadja (1995)* and Abel Ferrara's *The Addiction (1995)*, picked up the film for U.S. theatrical distribution in early 1996 as *Cemetery Man*.

By the time Aristide Massacessi had produced Michele Soavi's stunning debut feature *Stage-fright*, he was already a veteran of nearly forty years in the film business. Massacessi reportedly chose the D'Amato pseudonym because he thought it sounded more Italian-American and

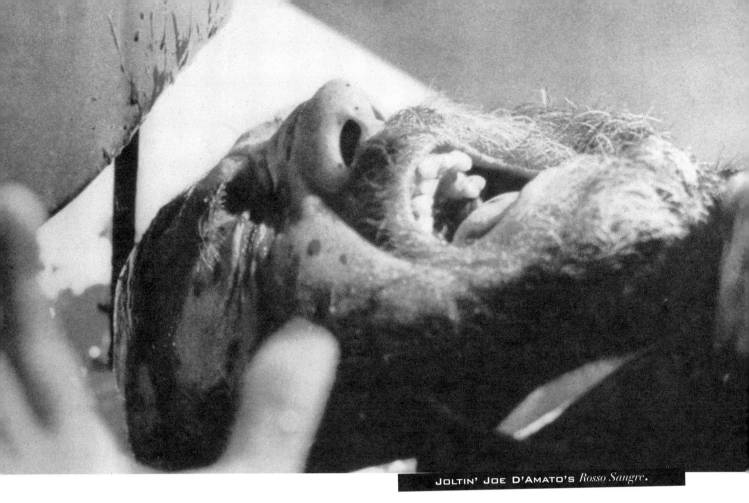

thus, more commercial. He claims to have originally spotted the name on a calendar. He's also employed such *nom de plumes* as Michael Wortuba, Steven Benson, Peter Newton, David Hills and Kevin Mancuso on dozens of films ranging from hardcore porno to sword 'n' sandal spectacles to gleefully outrageous splatfests. He often uses several pseudonyms on a single film because he performs multiple roles: director, producer, cinematographer, special makeup FX, editor or electrician. At fifteen, Massacessi was already working with his father at a film studio and apprenticing as as assistant camera operator. He was a cinematographer on Mario Bava's *Hercules in the Center of the World (1961)* and also worked with Bava's father, Eugenio, who engi-

neered the special effects on the film.

One of his first films as a director was the controversial, surreal and violent murder mystery, *La morte sorride all'assassino (1966)* (aka *Death Smiles on a Murderer*) starring Klaus Kinski. Massacessi also shot Alberto De Martino's *The Antichrist (1972)* (aka *The Tempter*) and continued producing and directing a series of Black Emanuelle films with Laura Gemser including *Emanuelle in Bangkok (1975)*, the infamous *Brutal Nights (1976)* (aka *Emanuelle in America*) and *Emanuelle and the Last Cannibals (1977)* (aka *Trap Them and Kill Them*).

Massacessi hit paydirt in the gore sweepstakes with a series of ultra-violent potboilers like *Buried Alive (1979)* (aka *Bui Omega, Beyond the Darkness*), *Anthropophagus (1979)* (aka *The Savage Island, The*

Grim Reaper) and the bloody sequel, *Monster Hunter (1981)* (aka *Horrible, Absurd, Anthropophagus 2*). Though U.S. audiences were treated to an edited version of *Anthropophagus* (as *The Grim Reaper* it was shorn of the fetus-eating scene, some of the graphic murders and nearly all the auto-cannibalism), *Buried Alive* arrived on these shores somewhat intact. Thriller Video crowed that it was "one of the most violent films ever made" and paired it with Umberto Lenzi's notorious *Make Them Die Slowly*. Horror hostess/poseur/parasite Elvira, simply refused to promote either title and would not appear to introduce the films as part of her ongoing series. Further controversy over whether real corpses were used in the film's graphic and painfully realistic autopsy and crematorium scenes (a charge Massacessi adamantly denies) only increased its demand among discriminating gorehounds everywhere. Massacessi has consistently explained that no real corpses actually appear in the film and that all the gory splatter effects were accomplished with "loads of internal organs purchased from a local butcher shop."

When *The Grim Reaper* became a modest financial success, Massacessi re-titled one of his later films, *Monster Hunter*, as *Anthropophagus 2/Grim Reaper II* to capitalize on the title's appeal. Luigi Montefiore (aka George Eastman), a hulking, hirsute humanoid, appears in both films and had previously worked with Massacessi as a writer, co-producer, director, star and even sex stud on such perverse delights as *Porno Holocaust (1979)*, *Emanuelle's Revenge (1975)* and *Erotic Nights of the Living Dead (1983)*. More polished than *The Grim Reaper* but equally inane, *Monster Hunter* pits Montefiore against an obsessed, vigilante priest

convinced the big lug's an "immortal ghoul." Again, the splatter really matters: guts spill between bloodied fingers; surgical drills are shoved through necks; eyes are gouged-out and heads are either severed or yanked into ovens and baked to a bubbling crisp. Though some of the violence is indeed horrific, it's mostly shoddy FX work that packs little of the wallop of Massacessi's more realistically-themed and highly troubling *Brutal Nights/Emanuelle in America (1984)*.

Emanuelle, again played by Laura Gemser, is a sexy photographer enamored by a wealthy playboy who enjoys the aphrodisiacal properties of snuff films and taped loops of war atrocities. Some of the scratchy, black-and-white, simulated torture/murder footage screened by Mr. Twisted is shockingly realistic and more than enough to make one's skin begin to crawl. Paired with the ugly violence is plenty of ugly sex—including a hair-raising sequence featuring a naked, nubile young woman in heat and an aroused thoroughbred horse that's best left to the imagination.

Massacessi will never be a critic's darling. But he is, undeniably, a prolific, talented, opportunistic businessman who's also a one-man film studio. From *Orgasmo Infernali*, *Super Climax* and *Hard Sensations* to *Ator the Invincible*, *2020 Texas Gladiators* and *Caligula: The True Story*, Massacessi has clearly shot it all. When D'Amato died in 1998, he left his bloodied paw prints over an impressively prodigious body of work, whose cinematic merits will continue to fuel the arguments of countless fanboy chat room debates for years to come.

Ruggero Deodato's roots lie not with horror or exploitation filmmaking but with the neorealist,

CANNIBAL HOLOCAUST

REGIE RUGGERO DEODATO **MUSIQUE /MUZIEK RIZ ORTOLANI**

EASTMANCOLOR

cinema verite works of his early mentor, Roberto Rossellini (former paramour of Ingrid Bergman and father of Isabella (*Blue Velvet*) Rossellini). Controversial, exploratory and naturalistic in tone and content, films such as *Open City (1945)*, (*Roma Citta aperta*) *Germany Year Zero (1946)* and *Paisan (1946)* were shocking to Italian audiences unaccustomed to Rossellini's frank, forthright and quasi-documentary style. Deodato would later employ many of Rossellini's signature techniques in what is arguably, The Greatest Cannibal Film Ever Made, *Cannibal Holocaust (1979)*.

After a fulfilling apprenticeship, Deodato's own directorial career began rather unsteadily, with tepid, jungle-girl potboilers like *Gungula (1973)* showing little indication of the terrible power he would manifest with his later work. *Ultimi Mondo Cannibale (1976)* (aka *Last Cannibal World*, *Jungle Holocaust*), a solid, invigorating action-thriller supposedly based on a true account of an oil company expedition's confrontation with a Stone Age tribe living in isolation on Mindao Island, would only set the stage for a project that would continue to haunt Deodato for the rest of his career.

Cannibal Holocaust was filmed almost entirely on location in Colombia, South America, and based on a rugged, uncompromising script by Gianfranco Clerici (who also wrote *Last Cannibal World*). The film would both condemn and exploit the atrocious treatment given Third World natives by greedy colonial entrepreneurs. At the film's world premier, Deodato was literally chased out of Colombia as rumors spread that he had actually killed native Indios on camera while his crew watched helplessly. Shortly after *Cannibal Holocaust* premiered in his native Italy, a judge ordered the film sequestered. Later, Deodato was convicted under an old law forbidding animal cruelty. He was sentenced to several months in

IF ALL YOU LOST WAS YOUR LEG IN *Cannibal Holocaust*, YOU'D CONSIDER YOURSELF BLESSED.

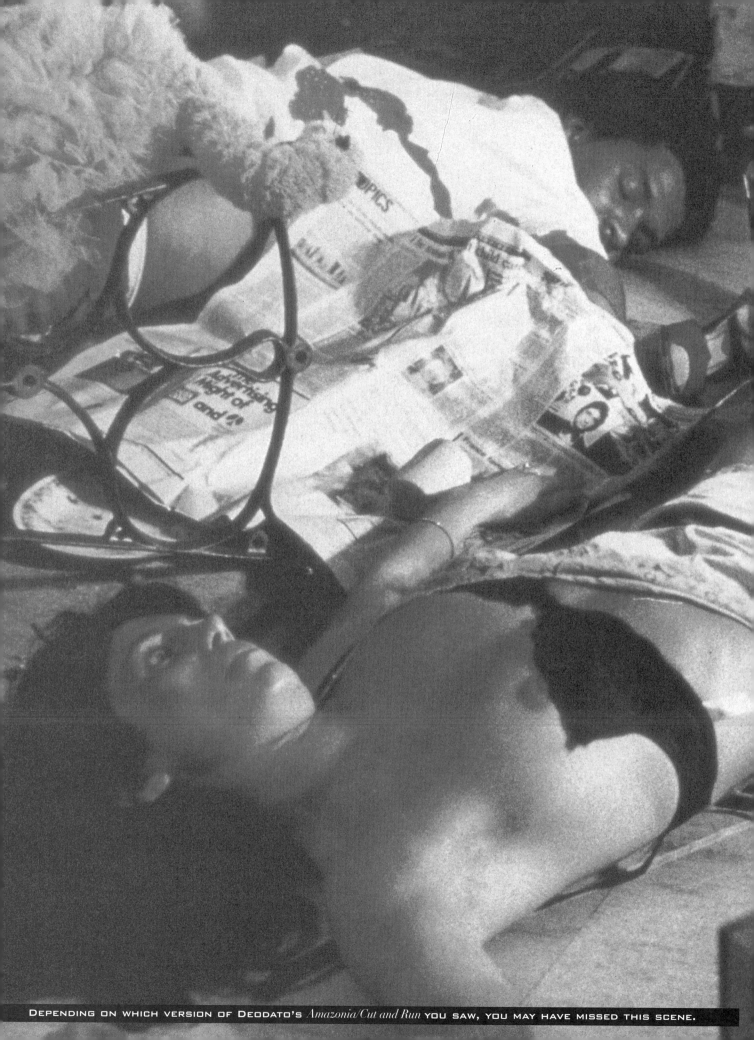

DEPENDING ON WHICH VERSION OF DEODATO'S *Amazonia/Cut and Run* YOU SAW, YOU MAY HAVE MISSED THIS SCENE.

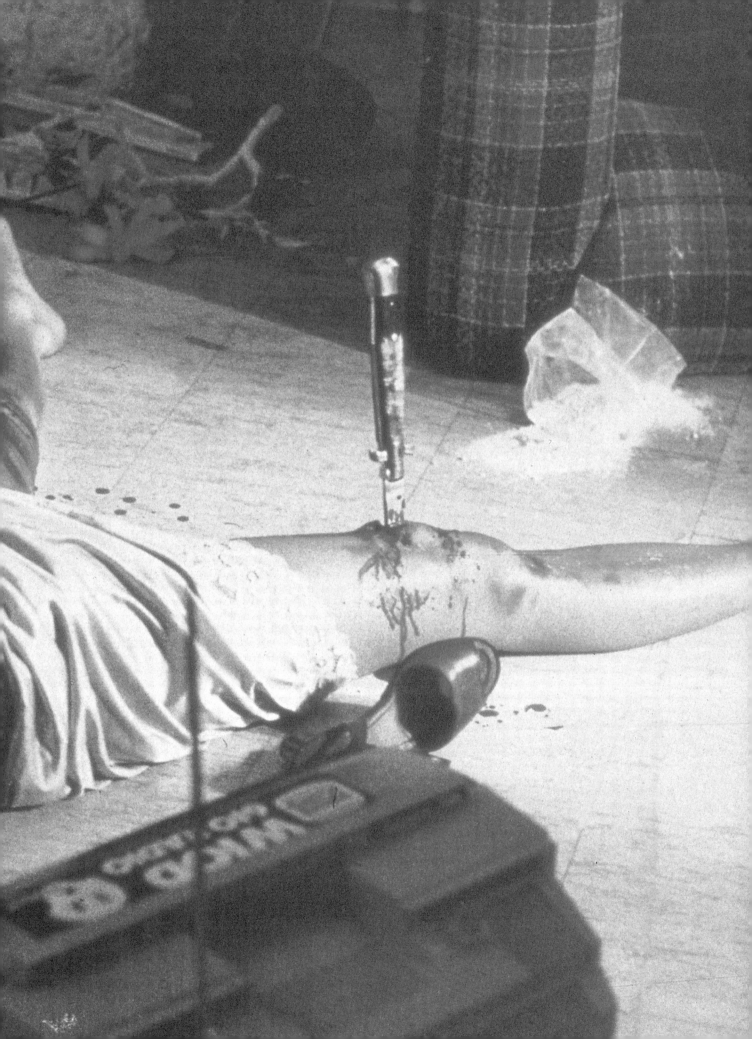

jail, probation, and forced to pay all expenses and legal fees. Deodato's professional reputation was sullied; he became a virtual pariah in the business and went without film work for years after the incident.

Despite a simmering controversy, several sequels (*Cannibal Holocaust 2*, *Cannibal Fury*, *Voodoo Revenge*) were planned but Deodato's return to the jungle four years later was to film *Inferno in diretta (1984)* instead. An action-adventure potboiler featuring Michael Berryman (one of the desert mutants in *The Hills Have Eyes*), the film was shot in two distinct versions for various foreign markets. A softer, sanitized version was released as *Cut and Run* in both the United States and Great Britain. A more graphic, violent cut (aka *Amazonia*) featuring gory stabbings, throat slittings, decapitations, eviscerations and a stunning, full-body bisection by jungle booby trap was released elsewhere.

Deodato began dabbling in science fiction with *Predatori d'Atlantide (1983)* (aka *Atlantis Interceptors*), a workmanlike *Mad Max*-on-the-water yarn before returning to the urban jungle found in the chilling, brutal *House on the Edge of the Park (1984)*. David Hess, the psycho-thug from Wes Craven's *Last House on the Left* (Hess also

essays a nearly identical role in the rarely seen *Hitch Hike (1978)* with Franco Nero), torments, humiliates, and scares the holy shit out of a group of jaded and bored party yuppies who'd picked him up to enliven their evening. Giovanni Lombardo Radice (aka John Morghen, Pasta-Land's favorite cinematic whipping boy) is the blithering, infantile sidekick: a twisted, comic foil to Hess' Hell-comes-to-your-house persona.

Far less effective was Deodato's slasher-come-lately, the teen-kill opus *Camping del terrore (1986)* (aka *Body-count*), a by-the-numbers stalka-thon whose main distinctions in-cluded its casting of a trio of genre vets: David Hess; Mimsy (*Four Flies on Grey Velvet*) Farmer; and Ivan (*Deep River Savages*) Rassimov, and its pounding Claudio Simonetti score. Again squandering his considerable talents, Deodato directed *The Barbarians (1986)*, a dopey, knuckle-headed sword 'n' sandal timewaster starring a pair of musclebound twins and legions of mono-syllabic party dogs.

Phantom of Death (1987), starring Michael York as a classical concert pianist suffering from a devastating, degenerative disease and prone to fits of homicidal rage, marked a marginal return to the genre. Written by frequent collaborator

Gianfranco Clerici; co-starring Donald Pleasence and John Morghen; and propelled by a pulsating score by Pino (*The Howling*) Dinaggio, *Phantom of Death* still proves terminally anemic despite a couple of showy kills and some bravura camera work.

Dial Help (1989), a somewhat kinky, slightly erotic non-thriller about possessed telephones, lethal ceiling fans and the "love/hate energies" trapped within electrical circuitry sounds just about as stupid as it plays. Fortunately, the film does showcase several leggy, fetching ingenues in state-of-the-art lingerie moaning, writhing and undulating in unfettered commitment to their craft. Deodato then directed the limply titled *The Washing Machine* (1993), yet another alleged "erotic thriller" that is a twisted triumph of sex over

sauce. The jury remains out for one of Italy's most perplexing directors.

Umberto Lenzi no longer enjoys talking about many of the films that made him famous. He acknowledges the fact that his three cannibal films (*Deep River Savages*, *Cannibal Ferox*, *Eaten Alive by the Cannibals*) put him on the splatmap, but he prefers directing crime thrillers, war movies, westerns or action-adventures. Lenzi still works in the genre, but has repeatedly protested, "I hate those (cannibal) movies." Along with Sergio Martino, Lenzi is one of the most prolific and most consistent of PastaLand auteurs. He is no stranger to any genre and has experienced success with a broad range of offerings: *Hell Below Deck* (1961) (a pirate adventure); *So Sweet, So Perverse* (1969); *Orgasmo* (1968); *From Hell to Victory* (1979); and *Violent*

Protection (1976). He has worked frequently in the past in the giallo tradition with works like *Eyeball (1974)*, *Paranoia (A Quiet Place to Kill) (1970)*, *Spasmo (1974)*, and *Seven Blood-Stained Orchids (1972)*.

When Lucio Fulci's *Zombie* answered the call of the undead sent out by Romero's *Dawn of the Dead*, Lenzi came back with *Incubo sulla Citta Contaminta (1980)* (released Stateside as both *Nightmare City* and *City of the Walking Dead*). Never one to miss an opportunity to slip in a door that others have opened, Lenzi also helmed horror knockoffs like *La Casa 3 (1988)* (aka *Ghosthouse*), *Welcome to Spring Break (1989)* (aka *Nightmare Beach*) and *Hitcher in the Dark (1989)*. In fact, you've probably seen several Lenzi films you weren't even aware of; he's used the *nom de plumes* Harry Kirkpatrick, Hank Milestone, Humphrey Humbert, Humphrey Logan and Bert Lenzi on dozens of titles.

Antonio Margheriti is yet another Italian director whose versatility, productivity and longevity are a testimonial to his journeyman-like work ethics. Frequently employing the pseudonym "Anthony M. Dawson," Margheriti's first forays into directing included both science fiction and horror: *Il Pianetta degli Uomoni Spenti (1963)* (aka *Battle of the Worlds*); *I Criminali della Galassia (1966)*; and *La Vergine di Norimberga (1963)* (aka *Virgin of Nuremberg*). Though often sited as a film that owes a great debt to both Maria Bava's *La Maschera del Demonio (1960)* and Roger Corman's *Pit and the Pendulum (1961)*, Margheriti's *Virgin of Nuremberg* is still vividly remembered for its mean-spirited cruelty and notorious torture sequences. The scene in which a cageful of hungry rats is placed over a screaming woman's face still retains its perverse and excruciating power to this day.

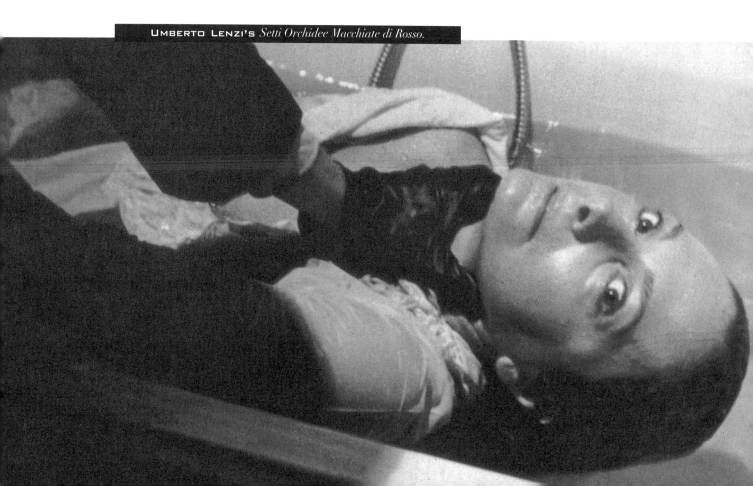

UMBERTO LENZI'S *Setti Orchidee Macchiate di Rosso.*

Two of his most successful and well-received genre efforts include a pair of nicely crafted, atmospheric gothic thrillers both starring horror icon Barbara Steele: *I Lunghi Capelli della Morte* *(1964)* (aka *Long Hair of Death*) and *La Danza Macabra* *(1964)* (aka *Castle of Blood*). Margheriti then directed *Nude...si Muore* *(1967)* (aka *School Girl Killer*), a routine whodunit about murders in a young girl's finishing school (surprise!) and the giallo thriller *La Morte Negli Occhi del Gatto* *(1972)* (aka *7 Deaths in a Cat's Eye*).

Though disputed by some and refused credit in many film reference books, Margheriti is listed as the director of both *Dracula Cerca Sangue* *(1973)* (aka *Andy Warhol's Dracula*) and *Il Mostro E in Taxola...Barone Frankenstein* *(1973)* (aka *Andy Warhol's Frankenstein*) in Phil Hardy's seminal *Encyclopedia of Horror Movies* (Harper-Row, NY). Paul Morrissey, a young Warhol acolyte, is usually credited as the director in most publications, though Italian sources insist that he merely provided the script and acted only in a "supervisory" capacity on both films.

Just as *Dawn of the Dead* inspired Fulci's *Zombie*, Lenzi's *City of the Walking Dead* and Bruno Mattei's *Hell of the Living Dead*, Margheriti's own *Apocalisse Domani* *(1980)* features Vietnam-era cannibals raising hell and gnoshing flesh in urban Atlanta, Georgia. An Italian-Spanish production shot on location with an Italian and American cast and crew, this unjustly maligned horror thriller has been released under a plethora of mouth-watering titles: *The Cannibals Are in the Streets*, *Savage Apocalypse*, *The Slaughterers* and *Cannibals in the City*.

U.S. audiences were faced with the truncated, relatively splatfree version of *Invasion of the Flesh Hunters*; while the Japanese import laser disc ver-

DEODATO'S LAME SLASHER, *Body Count*, WAS YEARS LATE IN THE TEENKILL SWEEPSTAKES.

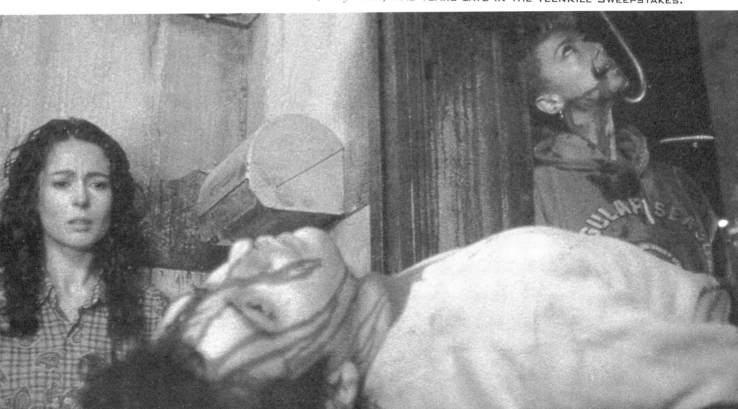

sion (and later, the DVD release) shows *Cannibal Apocalypse* in all its wide-screen, uncut glory. The exceptionally gory, rowdy FX sequences (by Fulci stalwart Gianetto de Rossi) missing from the U.S. print include: a vicious tongue biting scene in a hospital; a prolonged, splashy bit of mayhem involving a surgical bone saw; and the eye-popping *piece de resistance* — the daylight-through-John Morghen's-thorax effect that climaxes a bloody sewer shootout. There's plenty o'meat beneath the manholes of this muscular, cannibal chunkblower. Find the uncut version and become a Believer.

In Phil Hardy's otherwise excellent *Encyclopedia of Horror Movies*, Margheriti's violent Vietnam war epic *The Last Hunter (1980)* is incorrectly listed as merely another alternate title to *Cannibal Apocalypse*. In fact, the film, a straightforward action-thriller starring genre vets David (*The Beyond*) Warbeck and Tisa (*Zombie, Anthropophagus*) Farrow owes a substantial debt to both Michael Cimino's *The Deer Hunter (1978)* and Francis Coppolla's *Apocalypse Now (1979)*. Warbeck is an allied commando who's captured behind enemy lines and tortured by the Viet Cong. Farrow is the photographer. There are numerous bloody gun battles, suicides, killer rats, and several gory deaths by jungle booby traps. Lots of things get blown up. Warbeck dies a hero.

Sergio Martino, primarily known to U.S. audiences as the man behind such forgettable fare as *Screamers (1979)* and *Slave of the Cannibal God (1978)* (both films were heavily cut and re-edited for Stateside release) had already established himself as one of the real pioneers of the stalk-and-slash craze years before *Friday the 13th* made

the bodycount flick a force to be reckoned with. *Blade of the Ripper (1970)*, *Tail of the Scorpion (1971)*, *Day of the Maniac (1972)*, *Gently Before She Dies (1972)* and *Torso (1972)* unequivocally proved that Martino had been there...and done that already.

It would be grossly unfair and unforgivably negligent to ignore the contributions of many other Italian filmmakers whose early works helped define the modern horror film. Riccardo Freda, frequently hailed as "the first Maestro of Italian horror," was active in the genre in the '50s. His *I, Vampiri (1957)* (aka *The Devil's Commandment*) is often referred to as the film that kick-started the entire Italian horror film business. Though Freda usually receives full director's credit, he did not finish the film. When he departed several days short of completion, his cinematographer, Mario Bava, stepped in to wrap things up. The rest, as they say, is history. No?

Freda opted for an Anglo-sounding pseudonym (Robert Hampton) on the ridiculous *Caltiki: The Immortal Monster (1957)* before directing his much acclaimed, gothic masterpiece *L'Orribile Segnetto del Dr. Hichcock (1962)* (aka *The Horrible Dr. Hichcock*). Freda continued his obsessive, atmospheric and compelling genre explorations with *The Witch's Curse (1962)* and its sequel *The Ghost (1963)* (aka *Lo Spettro*) before directing the erotic thriller, *A Doppia Faccia (1969)* (aka *Double Face*) starring Klaus Kinski. The film, co-scripted by Lucio Fulci, bombed in Europe and was later padded with hardcore sex scenes and rereleased as *Heat and Joy* in 1976. *The Iguana with a Tongue of Fire (1971)* and the haunting *Follia Omicida (1980)* (aka *Murder Obsession, Fear*) ended Freda's most productive period. Today, in his 80s, he continues to work in films as a production consultant.

Mario Bava, a towering presence in early Italian cinema, produced an incredible body of work in his lifetime and his influence on the contemporary horror film cannot be overemphasized. Just as *Black Sunday (1960)* defined the gothic thriller and films like *Blood and Black Lace (1964)*, *Hatchet for the Honeymoon (1969)* and *Twitch of the Death Nerve (1972)* established the template for the stalk 'n' slash subgenre, Bava's other work proves a treasure trove for serious genre aficionados. *The Whip and the Body (1963)*, *Planet of Vampires (1964)*, *Kill Baby Kill (1966)* (aka *Operazione Paura, Curse of the Living Dead*), *Five Dolls for an August Moon (1970)*, *Lisa and the Devil (1972)* and *Baron Blood (1972)* are all part of an enduring legacy that remains rarely, if ever, challenged by contemporary genre filmmakers. Sadly, this great maestro was often reduced to directing such drive-in flotsam as *Dr. Goldfoot and the Girl Bombs (1966)* in order to survive the frequent down turns in his mercurial career. His influence and style continue to educate and impress genre filmmakers to this day. And, every Italian horror director working now is walking the path first paved by Mario Bava.

The Italian tradition in genre filmmaking is, indeed, a unique and rich blend of the traditional, the experimental and the derivative. The

Italians have invented some subgenres, stolen others, and recycled themes that somehow can seem new and fresh again. In many ways, the Italian film industry has treated the genre with a degree of respect, admiration and reverence, even. Traits conspicuously absent in most of the cynical and profit-hungry maneuverings of their Stateside counterparts. In a genre fraught with deceit, hype, hopeless sequels and intellectual blight, the Italians remain True Believers.

Viva il rosso...il profondo rosso!

JASON VOORHEES SAVORS HIS "TOP OF THE FOOD CHAIN" STATUS THROUGH
TEN BLOODY EPISODES OF THE *Friday the 13th* FRANCHISE.

The cHUnkbLoWers

There exists a shadowy, scurrilous mutant sub-genre lurking within the confines of the horror world. One in which only completists, the morbidly curious or the most hardcore need apply. It is a domain of wretched excess. Without limits. It's credo is "anything worth doing is worth *over* doing."

These are films that fester in a world beyond simple splatter and beyond gore. They are alternately reviled, banned and busted...or celebrated, collected and crowed about. Their appearances in public theatres are rare and the availability of many titles on commercial videocassette is spotty at best. Most people cannot even sit through one of them. These are the chunkblowers, the *ce ne plus ultra* of the Splatter film.

By their very nature, horror films encompass many of the most unpleasant, terrifying and repulsive elements of a life on the edge. They are forever pushing the parameters further and fur-ther away from smug complacency. The horror film enjoys a time-honored tradition of frightening, challenging, provoking and confounding its audiences. It is the bad dog of the cinematic world. It will not be tamed; it won't do tricks for you. Some films want to make you feel really shitty about yourself, mankind in general and the world around you. They'd just as soon piss on your leg as look at you.

The horror film explores the darkest nether regions of the human soul. It wants us to see the monsters and demons both within and without. It wants us to be afraid...very afraid.

"The oldest and strongest emotion of mankind is fear," said H.P. Lovecraft, "and the oldest and strongest kind of fear is fear of the unknown." The horror film is fiendishly designed to exploit that emotion for all it's worth.

But there is a certain element in horror film-making that refuses to be satisfied by simply scar-

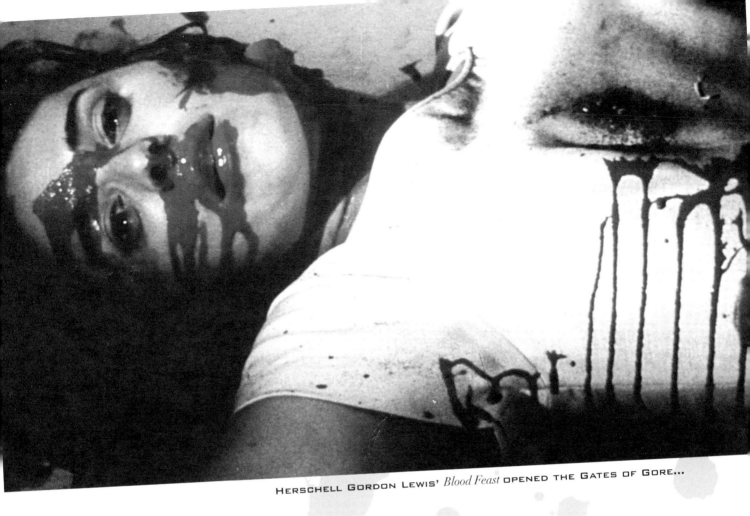

HERSCHELL GORDON LEWIS' *Blood Feast* OPENED THE GATES OF GORE...

ing, shocking or upsetting its viewers. They want more...much more. Many filmmakers want to push it as far as the law allows...and then some. They want to take you places you're not sure you want to go. Some want you to blow lunch.

Since blood is an essential lubricant in genre filmmaking anyway, the splatter film only exploited and extrapolated an ingredient that had been *de rigeur* since day one. But something began happening in the early '60s, when many filmmakers decided to discover for themselves if more was, indeed, better. In many cases, the decision to exponentiate the sanguinary quotient grew from simple economic necessity. Most horror films were marginally budgeted, lacking major stars and without much of the clout that mainstream

filmmakers enjoyed. Many needed some sort of gimmick in order to be noticed at all.

Herschell Gordon Lewis and David Friedman, small-time producers of black-and-white nudie flicks and other exploitation fare, found that gimmick and used it by the bucketful. *Blood Feast (1963)* was, by most accounts, a plodding, boring, ineptly acted and directed mess; featuring, perhaps, one of the most dreadful, brain-numbing "musical scores" ever composed for a feature film. But...there was blood, lots of it, and in garish color, too. But there was far more than just blood this time. There were dismemberments, tongue removals and splattered brains...all over the place. The gore scenes were shot like porno inserts, up close, explicit and clinically revealing. The film

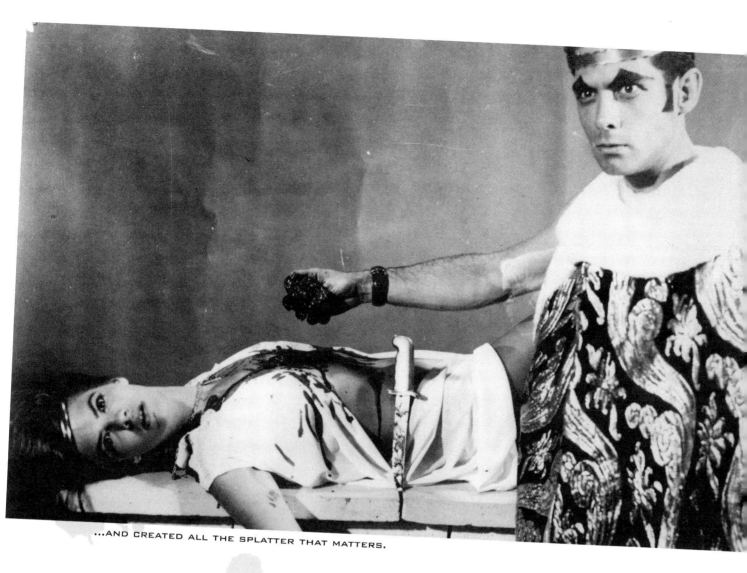

...AND CREATED ALL THE SPLATTER THAT MATTERS.

created a furor. Then a sensation. Then it made lots of money. *Blood Feast* was not really much of a horror film. It wasn't scary or suspenseful and the plot was barely recognizable. It was full of inane dialog, pedestrian performances and embarrassing moments of melodramatic ineptitude. But, it was wet...very, very wet. Not really horror, but gore. Perhaps the first real splatter film. The world had never seen anything quite like it before.

Lewis and Friedman repeated their winning recipe with *2000 Maniacs (1964)*, *Gruesome Twosome (1967)*, *A Taste of Blood (1967)*, *Wizard of Gore (1970)* and *The Gore Gore Girls (1972)*. All featured a generous slate of interpersonal fleshen mayhem:

beheadings, dismemberments, eviscerations, scalpings, torture, death by knife, sawblade, spike, axe and drill press. The floodgates were opened and nothing would staunch that flow for the next 3o years.

The producers and distributors of the German-made *Hexen Bis Auf Blut (1969)* (*Witches Tortured Till They Bleed*) copped a riff or two from the theatrical and carnival-style antics of hucksters Lewis and Friedman by retitling their film *Mark of the Devil* and offering "stomach distress bags" for what they cried was the "first film rated 'V' for violence!" The tortures, rapes, burnings, tongue-yankings and piercings were not as graph-

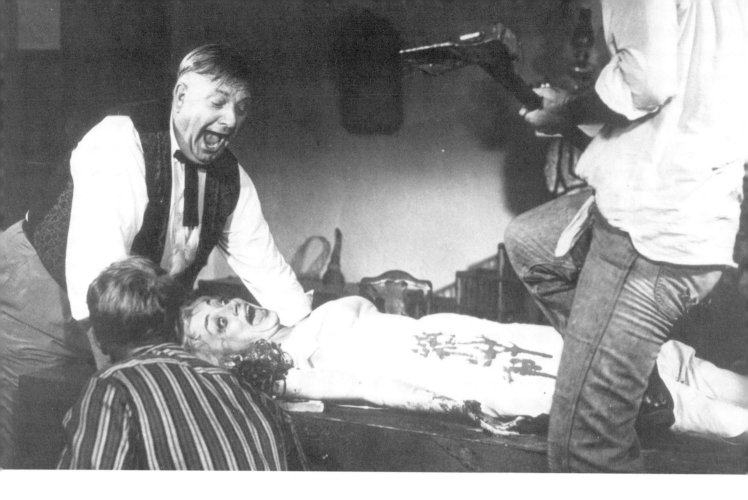

No, they don't take too kindly to strangers in these parts—
unwelcome whacks from card-carrying members of the clan from *2000 Maniacs*.

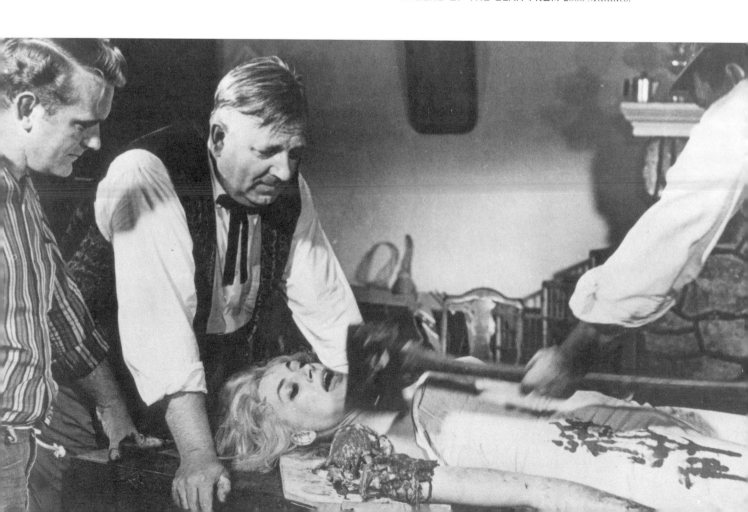

WEASEL AND SADIE WERE ON THEIR WAY TO A KILLER PARTY
AT THE *Last House on the Left.*

DIRECTOR WES CRAVEN
ALWAYS KNEW...
it's only a movie...only a movie.

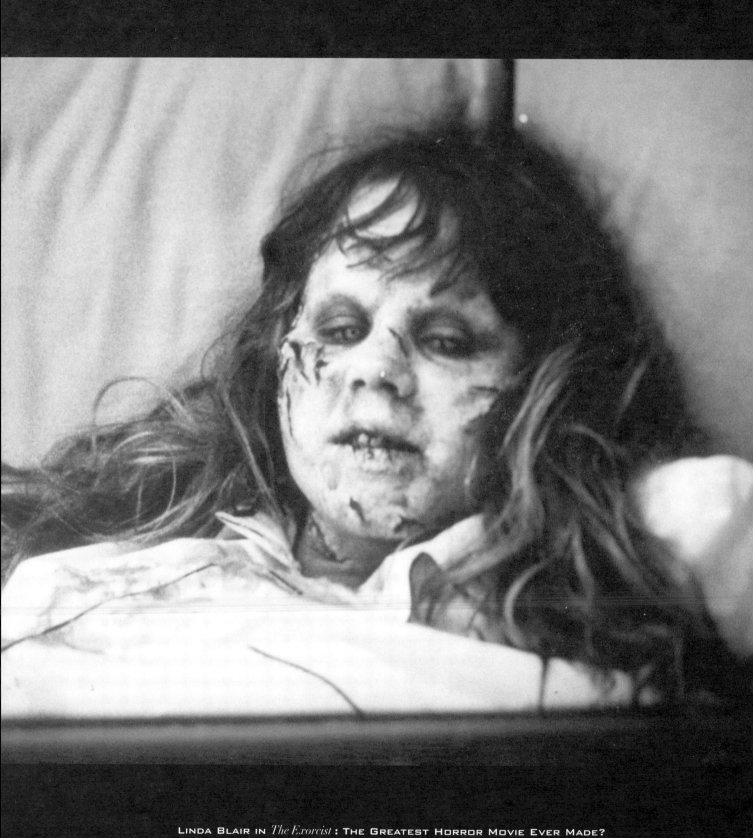

LINDA BLAIR IN *The Exorcist* : THE GREATEST HORROR MOVIE EVER MADE?

ic as Lewis'; but an extremely clever and wily advertising campaign made you believe you were going to leap out of your skin and lose your cookies while viewing the film. However, one of the film's stars, the creepy, skeletal and crater-faced Reggie Nalder, nearly accomplished both goals singlehandedly, and all without makeup or effects.

The same formula (which already had cribbed mightily from Michael Reeve's superlative *Witchfinder General (1968)*) was employed again in a sequel *Mark of the Devil II (1972)* with little success.

Wes Craven's *Last House on the Left (1972)* pushed cinematic sadism to the limit, but without the explicit graphic excesses of the Lewis' films. Many viewers still insist they saw more than they really did. Even today, Craven is unsure just what version most people witnessed in 1972. He has admitted that both he and producer Sean Cunningham reedited the film after its initial release and also acknowledges that many theatre owners cut the film again to their own specifications. Vestron released a supposedly uncut, 85-minute print of the film on videocassette in 1985, but an even longer version later surfaced on a Japanese laser disc in letterboxed format. MGM released what is widely believed to be the most complete version now available on DVD in 2002.

Both Italian and Spanish filmmakers began to add a little extra sauce to their features, too. Mario Bava's bloody and ultraviolent *Twitch of the Death Nerve (1972)* established the blueprint for the stalk 'n' slash/bodycount flick while Paul Naschy's *Horror Rises from the Tomb (1972)* and *Hunchback of the Morgue (1972)* spilled their guts with a bravura

platter of heart removals, human sacrifices, garden tool murders and flaming rat attacks.

Even mainstream films began to up the splatter ante a bit and more than just a handful of theatres reeked of puke and tossed cookies when the next audience sat down for William Friedkin's *The Exorcist (1973)*. This was a genuine and brutal shocker based on William Peter Blatty's runaway bestseller. It is as intense today as it was over 30 years ago. It remains entirely speculative that the film, if released today, would even be remotely considered for the lenient "R" rating it received upon its initial release. Despite its graphic crucifix masturbation scene; the 360 degree head swivel; the bruised and pus-flecked appearance of Regan; the pea-soup hurling; and levitation sequence, the most striking special effect remains Dick Smith's sublime old-age makeup worn by Max Von Sydow. He was only 43 years old when he accepted the titular role.

Andy Warhol's Frankenstein (1973), directed by Antonio (*Cannibal Apocalypse*) Margheriti and "supervised" by Paul Morrissey, was one of the very few films to ever receive an MPAA "X" certification, more for gore and violence rather than for sexual explicitness. It is a goofy, tasteless, bawdy and taboo-trashing gore-comedy about an incestuous necrophile attempting to create a master race in his laboratory. It was also probably the only real chunkblower to ever receive a theatrical release in 3D. Few patrons will ever forget the final soliloquy delivered by an impaled Udo Keir, who rambles eloquently amidst a gory pile of dismembered limbs and eviscerated bodies while his own speared liver dangles precariously at least 20 feet out over the heads of the audience.

Soon, a new wave emanating from Italian shores was to forever change the face of the gore film. Perhaps taking a clue from a series of sensationalistic pseudo-documentaries like *Mondo Cane* *(1961)*, *Mondo Bizarro (1965)*, Jacopetti and Prosperi's *Africa Addio (1966)*, and Paolo Cavara's *The Wild Eye (1968)*, several filmmakers began using actual footage of real life slaughter scenes for inclusion in their otherwise fictional scenarios. Ruggero Deodato's *The Last Cannibal World* *(1976)* (aka *The Last Survivor, Jungle Holocaust*) showed a crocodile being slowly skinned alive, a loathsome genre innovation that was to be sickeningly repeated in a series of ultra-violent third world cannibal films for the next half decade.

Joe D'Amato's *Emmanuelle and the Last Cannibals (1977)* (aka *Trap Them and Kill Them*) showed breasts being eaten, penises cut off, intestines ripped out and bodies lovingly bisected. (In this case, Donald O'Brien's...soon to become *Dr. Butcher, M.D.*)

Sergio Martino's *Slave of the Cannibal God* *(1978)* initially proved rather tepid, in a lackluster tale of a woman (Ursula Andress) in search of her missing explorer-husband, presumed lost and dead in the jungles of New Guinea. But the uncut version, *Mountain of the Cannibal God*, reveals a generous and reprehensible slate of real animal atrocity footage inserted throughout.

The Grand Slam of Cannibal Carnage was now just around the corner. Inarguably the best and most provocative of the bunch, Ruggero Deodato's *Cannibal Holocaust (1979)* proves a flawed masterpiece, ultimately undone by its own swaggering sense of cynicism and hypocrisy. When a group of cocky young, amoral hotheads attempt to document their search for a missing expedition lost in the Amazon, they find a hostile, unforgiving jungle hell, where even the fittest don't survive. Again, there is an alarming amount of animal slaughter: huge turtles are hacked apart and gutted; monkey's skulls are split and their brains eaten; others are shot, beaten and eviscerated in loving close-up. Deodato has offered a feeble defense that all the animals killed on screen were later eaten, but the careful staging and camera-friendly nature of their executions remains inexcusable. Of course, the humans fare no better, but at least they could still get up and have lunch after their scene was in-the-can.

Nearly as soon as the new expedition arrives, they witness a native repeatedly thrusting a sharp stone dildo into his adulterous wife's vagina until she expires. Later a pregnant woman has her fetus manually aborted and then buried in the mud. Another young Amazonian girl is impaled, from ass-through-mouth, upon an 8-foot sharpened wooden stake. The film lurches to its climax as the expedition is surrounded and killed off, one by one. The woman is gang raped, beheaded and then eviscerated. One of the men has his penis cut off moments before he's hacked into pieces by stone axes. Deodato ran into some legal complications once he returned home, as many of his detractors insisted that many of the scenes involving human slaughter were, in fact, real. That charge has never been satisfactorily proven, but several prints of the film were mysteriously destroyed in the wake of the litigation. Deodato was eventually summoned to court to answer charges of animal cruelty and his career was put on hold for the next three years.

MACHETE MAYHEM AND
CRANIAL DETONATION FROM
GEORGE A. ROMERO'S HERCULEAN
ZOMBIE CHUNKBLOWER
Dawn of the Dead.

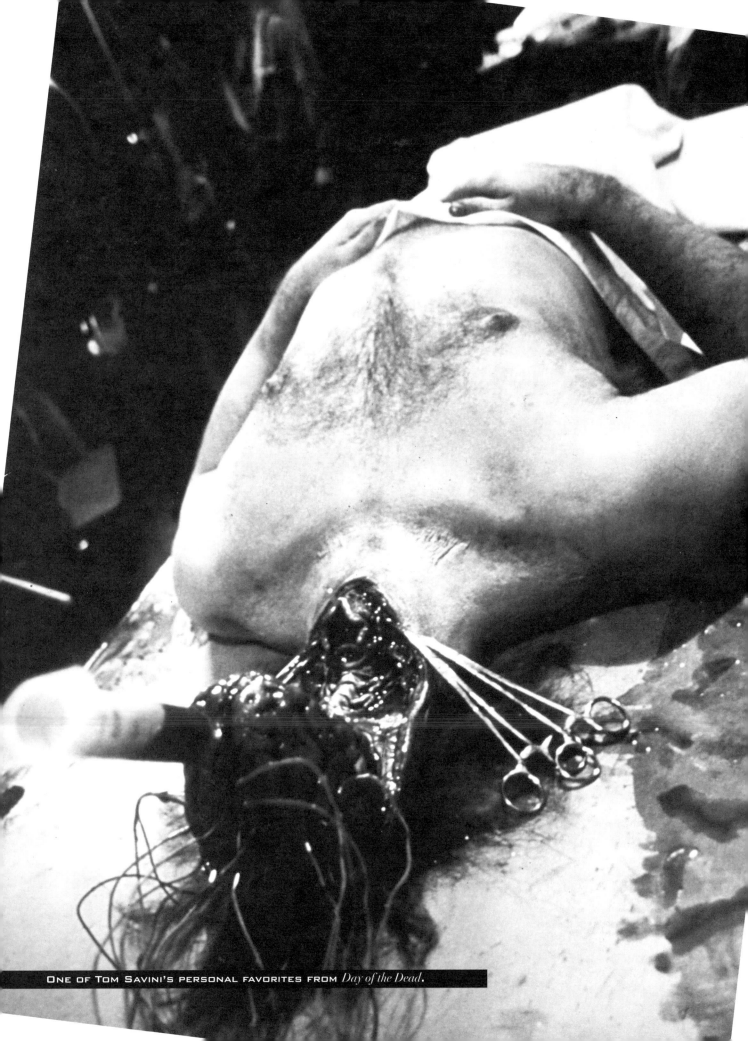

ONE OF TOM SAVINI'S PERSONAL FAVORITES FROM *Day of the Dead*.

Though the cannibal film was entering into eclipse at the beginning of the decade, numerous rip-offs and shoddy knock-offs of Deodato's work still surfaced. Umberto Lenzi, who had jump-started the cannibal subgenre in 1972 with *Man From Deep River* (aka *Deep River Savages*), produced *Eaten Alive by the Cannibals (1980)* (aka *Doomed to Die, The Emerald Jungle*). Shamelessly

Lenzi rapidly followed with *Cannibal Ferox (1981)* (aka *Make Them Die Slowly*), a gut-churning Greatest Hits package of jungle atrocities, and Deodato added his final footnote to the cycle with *Amazonia (1984)* (aka *Inferno in diretta*). Deodato's film, released Stateside as *Cut and Run*, was a far more graphic gorefest in its original form before being sanitized for U.S. audiences. In *Amazonia*,

GORE GALORE IN *Day of the Dead*.

lifting footage from his previous films; borrowing a bit of loose "mondo" material; and pilfering the My My Lai beheading and evisceration sequence from Deodato's *Last Cannibal World*, Lenzi delivers a crazy-quilt amalgam of the sub-genre's greatest hits. Ivan Rassimov, star of Lenzi's *Man From Deep River*, returns as a messianic Jim Jones-type, leading a "purification sect" into the jungles of New Guinea where they distinguish themselves by their crafty use of dildos dipped in cobra venom.

nearly all the stabbings, spearings and machete mayhem were presented explicitly, though the *piece de resistance* remains the spectacular drawing and quartering of one hapless explorer snared in a jungle booby trap.

While the cannibal film was in full flower, several Stateside developments would herald a new wave of nastiness and brutality before George Romero's watershed film, *Dawn of the Dead (1979)* would kick down the doors of restraint forever.

Joel M. Reed's *Bloodsucking Freaks (1978)* would

enflame women's groups with its cheerfully misogynistic cavalcade of torture visited upon mostly nude women; but it would be the rarely-seen, pseudonymously-produced *Last House on Dead End Street (1977)* that would prove the most distressing. Clearly, things were changing now and moving in a frightful new direction. Supposedly produced by a group of New York film students and briefly titled both *The Fun House* and *Cuckooo Clocks from Hell*, *Last House on Dead End Street* is a profoundly disturbing, powerfully creepy examination of a morally bankrupt filmmaker and his twisted passion to make "some really weird films... something nobody ever dreamed of."

Those dreams rapidly become nightmares, as he begins filming a series of excruciatingly brutal snuff sequences for inclusion in his magnum opus. Despite their crude execution and low-tech special FX, these vicious and unsettling vignettes retain their twisted and perverse power to this day. One of the lucky ones is merely strangled and suffocated on camera. Another is forced to kneel and orally copulate a severed deer's hoof extruding from the crotch of a horned and topless cackling female. He is later dispatched via a Black and Decker impromptu lobotomy as he lies cowering and crying on the floor, begging for his life.

However, the most disturbing sequence (repeated throughout in flashback) is the prolonged and systematic surgical torture administered to a woman who has been drugged and bound to an ersatz operating table. Her face is repeatedly slashed with scalpels before a handsaw is employed to amputate her legs. Each time she loses consciousness, she is revived with smelling salts. Before she drifts off forever, though, her abdomen is opened by a pair of tin snips and she's thoroughly gutted. Her gleaming intestines are held high and passed around the room, accompanied by much sniggering laughter and back-slapping bravado. This is the *Last House* you'll want to visit for quite some time.

In 1979, Romero's *Dawn of the Dead* changed the face of splatter forever. As soon as that S.W.A.T team entered the zombie-infested apartment building, things would never, ever, be the same again. A burly, shotgun-toting cop huffs up to a closed door and sets himself in front of it. He kicks it down and, with it, all the accepted conventions of modern horror filmmaking. A male figure briefly confronts him before the shotgun roars, blowing the man's head into a crunchy red mist and right into splatter film history. Though no more explicit nor spectacular than any of the other gore set pieces throughout the film, it is the

JOE PILATO WILL SOON CHOKE ON MORE THAN JUST HIS WORDS.

THIS RAZOR-WIELDING CAPUCHIN

GETS STRAIGHT TO THE POINT IN

Monkeyshines: an Experiment in Fear.

LEFT: "BUB" MAY BE THE
EDUCATED SLIGHTLY
SOPHISTICATED ZOMBIE
IN *Day of the Dead*, BUT HE'S
STILL NO VEGETARIAN.

THEY'RE *definitely* COMING TO GET YOU DURING THE *Night of the Living Dead*.

positioning of that shocking sequence in the first few minutes that serves terrible notice of the film-maker's subversive intentions. The kicking down of that particular door served handily as a metaphor for the gruesome carnage to follow, both in the remaining film as well as in the upcoming decade. The floodgates were opened. There was no stopping the Crimson Tide.

Dawn of the Dead became an international suc-cess on many levels. Along with John Carpenter's *Halloween*, Romero's film became one of the most financially rewarding independent productions of all time, grossing well over $50 million during its theatrical run. Besides being adored and virtually enshrined by legions of horror fans, even the mainstream critics found much to admire. Roger Ebert gave it "four stars", calling it "one of the best horror films ever made...brilliantly crafted, funny, droll and savagely merciless." Others remarked on Romero's brutal parody of American consumer behavior, our frenzied shopping habits, and the addictive and possessive nature of our rampant obsession with material comforts. Even the extreme violence and wall-to-wall gore were dealt with rather dispassionately; *Dawn of the Dead* displays a wicked wit, healthy doses of black humor and frequently plants its rotted tongue firmly in its ravaged cheek.

THIS POINTLESS 1990 REMAKE OF *Night of the Living Dead* DIVIDED
THE FANS AND BIT ZOMBIE WAZOO AT THE BOX OFFICE.

Because the film established new levels of graphic on-screen mayhem, *Dawn of the Dead* made a star out of its special makeup effects artist, former combat photographer Tom Savini. Honing his chops on earlier proto-splatter projects like *Deathdream (1972)*, *Deranged (1974)* and *Martin (1977)*, Savini was enthroned as the reigning "King of Gore," a reputation that would alternately both help and haunt him for the following decade. Indeed, Savini pulled out all the stops in *Dawn*: heads were sheared by helicopter rotor blades, blown to bits by heavy weaponry and lopped off by machete. Limbs were routinely separated from their hosts, bodies were shredded

and guts were gobbled with mucho gusto. *Dawn of the Dead* ultimately did for the special makeup effects business what the Beatles and Rolling Stones did for the garage band.

Ripped-off repeatedly, but never duplicated, *Dawn of the Dead* was a towering achievement— still regularly screened, enthusiastically debated and coveted with an undying passion. At present, at least three distinct versions of the film are widely recognized: Romero's original, unrated 126-minute theatrical print; a slightly shorter European cut supervised by Italian co-producer Dario Argento; and a 141-minute, non-theatrical 16mm print circulated among various college

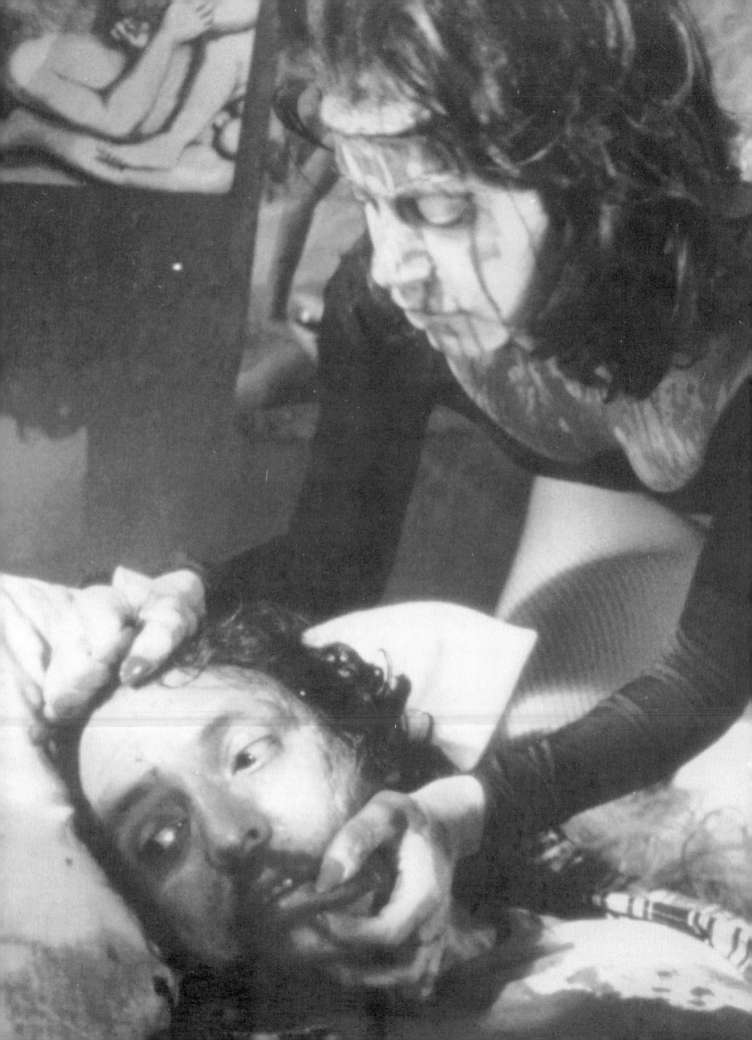

JOE SPINELLI IS ABOUT TO LOSE HIS NOGGIN IN *Maniac*. HE REALLY HOPES IT'S ONLY A BAD DREAM...

campuses during the early '80s.

Romero later sought to expand his cinematic horizons and decrease the emphasis on industrial-strength splatter with spotty success. *Knightriders (1980)*, *Creepshow (1982)*, *Monkeyshines: An Experiment in Fear (1988)* and *Two Evil Eyes (1991)* all performed below expectations. Romero resurrected his zombie army with *Dawn's* ultra gory and talkative follow-up, *Day of the Dead (1985)*, and then wrote and co-produced a misguided, pointless remake of *Night of the Living Dead (1990)*, directed by Tom Savini. Romero left zombies behind and helmed *The Dark Half (1993)*, based on the Stephen King bestseller, and *Bruiser (2001)*, a clunky loser about a guy who lost his face—and couldn't find it anywhere.

Savini continued his acting career after *Dawn* as well as supplying the sauce to such gore epics as *Friday the 13th (1980)*, *Maniac (1981)*, *The Burning (1981)*, *The Prowler (1981)* and *Friday the 13th IV: The Final Chapter (1984)*. He landed a major co-starring role in 1995 for Quentin (*Pulp Fiction*) Tarantino and Robert (*El Mariachi*) Rodriguez' apocalyptic vampire epic, *From Dusk 'Til Dawn (1996)*. But it was *Maniac*, a low budget, gorenographic blood feast directed by William Lustig and starring veteran character actor Joe Spinell, that was to bring unwanted notoriety to Savini's doorstep. Released without an MPAA rating, the film was lambasted by both critics and various women's groups for its relentless savagery. Savini himself has since expressed profound reservations about the extreme violence and vicious gore effects he executed: throats are slit; women are taunted, then humiliated before being stabbed and scalped; heads are torn-off and pulverized by shotguns,

ONE OF THE WOMEN *for* VIOLENCE IN WILLIAM LUSTIG'S CONTROVERSIAL *Maniac.*

and limbs amputated by machete. The "dramatic context" of these acts is perilously missing-in-action during the film, which seems to exist solely as a catalogue of hateful and gruesome carnage visited almost exclusively upon its female victims. The recently restored, letterboxed director's cut released on domestic laser disc by Elite Entertainment in 1995 did absolutely nothing to enhance the film's sullied reputation.

Both Savini and Romero's involvement with *Dawn of the Dead* would also ignite a firestorm of European interest in zombie slaughterfests: Lucio Fulci's *Zombie (1979)* (aka *Zombies 2*, *Zombie Flesh Eaters*); Umberto Lenzi's *City of the Walking Dead (1980)*; Andrea Bianchi's *Burial Ground (1980)* (aka *Zombie III*); Bruno Mattei's insufferable *Hell of the Living Dead (1981)* (aka *Zombie Creeping Flesh*, *Night of the Zombies*), and Frank Agrama's multi-

national *Dawn of the Mummy (1981)* would also showcase plenty of guts but little of the brains behind Romero's masterpiece. Of these directors, only Lucio Fulci exhibited any modicum of film-making savvy. He was incredibly prolific in the '80s and continued well into the '90s with an uneven, but always eclectic slate of films like *Murderock (1984)*, *The Devil's Honey (1986)*, *Aenigma (1987)*, *Demonia (1988)*, *House of Clocks (1989)*, *Door to Silence (1991)*, *Sodoma's Ghost (1988)*, *Touch of Death (1988)* and the long-delayed sequel to his breakthrough chunkblower, *Zombie 3 (1988)*. Fulci rarely skimps on the sauce, either, effectively utilizing the grisly skills of FX artists like Gianetto de Rossi, Franco Di Girolamo and Maurizio Trani to realize his blood-soaked visions. The release of *Un Gato Nel Cervello (1990)* (aka *A Cat in the Brain*, *Nightmare Concert*) caused an ecstatic rippling

JOE SPINELLI'S DEAD MOULDY MOM WANTS SOME ATTENTION.

effect amongst the gore *cognescenti*, as Fulci delivered what many considered his bloodiest effort to date. Scant attention was focused on the fact that Fulci shamelessly cribbed footage from several prior projects (most noticeably *Bloody Psycho*, *Touch of Death* and *Sodoma's Ghost*) as he gamely and bravely essayed the lead role of a horror film director plagued by nightmarish visions and hallucinations. This film has it all: cats feasting on pulsing human brains; bodies reduced to steak tartar and pigfood by chainsaw and meat grinder; and heads, limbs and guts pureed with a gleeful, wild abandon. Not too shoddy for a guy approaching seventy, eh?

Several other events in the '90s kept Fulci's name in the splatter spotlight. A 1994 re-release by Cine City (Holland) and Professional Cine Media of his Big Apple slasher, *Lo Squartatore di New York (1982)* (aka *The New York Ripper*) in an uncut, letterboxed laser disc version, revealed the film to be far nastier and gorier than its severely truncated Stateside counterpart. There is also more sex and casual nudity in the unexpurgated print, and the violence is both vicious and lingering. Justifiably accused of rampant misogyny, the camera lovingly dwells upon a woman's face, eyeball, breast and nipple being sliced by razorblade; others are dispatched by a quacking psychotic's frenzied knife attacks and throat slitting expertise. Yet another female victim has her vagina split open by a jagged, broken bottle and summarily gutted. The camera misses nothing. The final, climactic splatter tableau includes a splashy, blossoming exit wound erupting on the perpetrator's cheek as he's shot to death. It's practically an entirely different film than the one familiar to

U.S. audiences and the unedited violence remains shocking and ghastly, even to seasoned viewers.

Fulci continued to maintain a higher profile in the '90s by also appearing at numerous international horror film festivals and conventions and presenting his totally uncut, director's print of his unassailable zombie masterpiece, *The Beyond*, to adoring acolytes in Europe, England and the United States. He also signed on to direct a remake of the venerable *Mystery of the Wax Museum* in 1996, to be produced by Italian maestro Dario Argento, but died unexpectedly from complications of diabetes during pre-production.

Indeed, *Dawn of the Dead* was one of the most explosive of catalytic agents to burst upon the rapidly shifting genre scene in nearly a decade. However, two other developments occurring nearly simultaneously in the early '80s were to prove equally significant. Their impact continues to be felt and will easily resonate well into the next century. Summarily taken for granted by contemporary horror fans, these two factors, nonetheless, became crucial turning points in the metamorphosis of the modern splatter phenomenon. And, today, much like the music fan who's never owned a vinyl album nor ever seen a rock & roll movie on the big screen, the video revolution has been largely absorbed by the latest ultra-high tech gimmicks in the computer landscape. But in the early '80s, the videocassette player was to prove an essential link between an audience and the rarely-seen theatrical, genre, or foreign films that were previously only screened in arthouse

JOE, THIS SIMPLY ISN'T
GOING TO WORK *(Maniac)*.

TOM SAVINI'S FX IN *The Burning* MADE IT JUST A CUT ABOVE THE USUAL SLASHER FARE.

Friday the 13th Part V: A New Beginning WAS ANYTHING BUT.

cinemas, drive-ins or in severely edited form on commercial television.

The VCR became an extremely potent tool for horror audiences to connect with their favorite films...again and again. This revolution in technology rocked the boat even more so than the recent canonization of the Makeup Artist As Demigod. As films became even wetter, more realistic and simply outrageous, they were also seen more often by their target audience. People now accustomed to sophisticated animatronics, puppeteering, and state-of-the art computer graphics are frequently nonplussed at the startling impact of such seminal low-tech terrorfests as *The Texas Chainsaw Massacre*, *Friday the 13th*, *Halloween* or even the original *Alien*. After being raised on 150 gazillabyte cybertech terrors like *Aliens (1986)*, *Terminator 2 (1991)*, *Jurassic Park (1993)* or *Species (1995)*, such ear-

lier fare can seem positively prehistoric today. Oh...but there was a time...

Tom Savini, rapidly becoming an ancient warrior in a Brave New World populated by his own over-achieving proteges, has often lamented the fact that he was rarely asked to execute creature and fantasy effects. The producers all wanted splatter—and in increasingly large doses. Of course, today, you can easily get both in the very same film.

After a long and tiresome run of teenkill slasher flicks, maniac mayhem and graphic gorefests, films like *My Bloody Valentine (1981)*, *Pieces (1983)*, *The Prowler (1981)*, *Silent Night, Deadly Night (1983)* or any of the *Friday the 13th* sequels, were beginning to show their age. The makeup effects technologies had exponentially increased in a few short years, so every slit throat, severed appen-

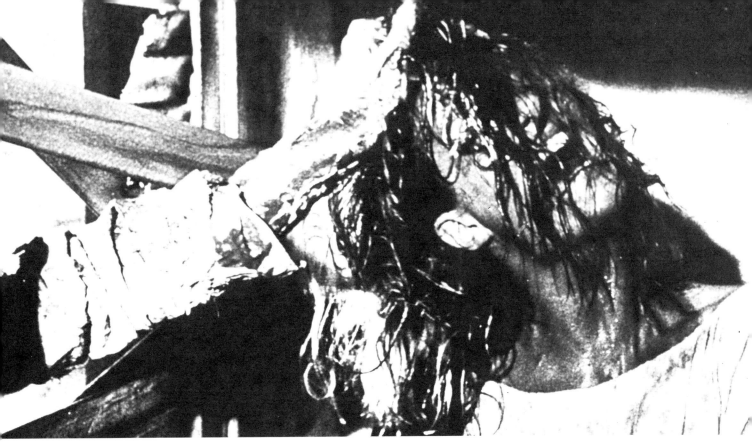

MOMENTS BEFORE THE "14" SPLINTER THE ROCKED THE WORLD"
FROM LUCIO FULCI'S PASTALAND CLASSIC, *Zombie.*

dage or crushed cranium looked alarmingly real, but the incessant bodycount bloodbath was becoming boring and predictable even to the most hardcore fans.

Two young makeup FX artists, one a student of the other, soon discovered an ideal splatter hybrid: the monster-gore film. Now, creatures of all sorts: aliens, werewolves, nuclear and chemical mutations, giant bugs or shape-shifting creepazoids could join the human carnage, increasing the splatter quotient tremendously. Bodies of all kinds could now be ripped apart with a brand new attitude.

Rick Baker, a young protege of makeup maestro Dick Smith, and his one-time assistant, Rob Bottin, were to give cinematic splatter an entirely new visage. Baker's work in *The Fury (1978)*, *An American Werewolf in London (1981)*, *Funhouse (1981)*

and *Videodrome (1983)*; and Bottin's contributions to *Piranha (1978)*, *Humanoids From The Deep (1980)*, *The Howling (1981)* and John Carpenter's *The Thing (1982)*, gave both monster and gore fans plenty to chew on. Baker's eclectic, fanciful work in *Videodrome*, easily one of the most sadly neglected, intelligent and sophisticated chunkblowers of the new era, still manages to retain its two-fisted, visceral punch. And Bottin's eye-popping, jaw-dropping and knee-slappin' creature splatter in *The Thing* still make that film, arguably, the mainstream's Wettest Film Ever. Both artists periodically strayed from strict genre assignments but still continued to amaze. Baker's effects in *Greystoke (1984)*, *The Incredible Shrinking Woman (1981)*, *Harry and the Hendersons (1987)* (Academy Award), *Gremlins 2 (1990)*, *Coming to America (1988)*, *Gorillas in the Mist (1988)*, *Wolf (1994)*, *Baby's Day Out (1994)*,

The Nutty Professor (1996) (another Oscar), *Men in Black (1997)*, *Mighty Joe Young (1998)* and *Men in Black II (2002)* showed continuous growth and experimentation. Bottin accepted fewer gigs, but they were all big-budget, mainstream films like *The Witches of Eastwick (1987)*, *RoboCop (1987)*, *Total Recall (1990)* (Academy Award), *Bugsy (1991)*, *Basic Instinct (1992)*, and David Fincher's controversial *Seven (1995)*.

Savini, Baker and Bottin, and the wet and florid coverage continually provided them by the world's most widely distributed genre publication, *Fangoria* magazine, all contributed to the legions of dedicated (and rabidly fanatical) FX artists who followed in their bloody footsteps. Many horror films in the mid-to-late '80s considerably upped the ante on the splat-o-meter by the infusion of all the fresh, new blood who were constantly experimenting with newer and more advanced technologies.

As films became wetter, they also became more eclectic and less dependent upon established formula. Sam Raimi's *Evil Dead 2: Dead by Dawn (1987)*, Wes Craven's *A Nightmare on Elm Street (1983)*, Jim Muro's *Street Trash (1987)*, and Peter Jackson's *Bad Taste (1987)* and *Dead Alive (1993)* all took splatter in various new directions and featured copious contributions by a variety of new effects artists. In a trend partially initiated by the complex demands of the gore/creature/fantasy elements in *Evil Dead 2*, many films began to employ multiple effects studios in order to accomplish their aim. It soon became obvious that very few FX houses could excel at all of the new technologies. Prosthetics, animatronics, motion-control, rear-screen and blue-screen

applications, puppeteering, miniature and model-making, matte painting, dental and optical enhancement, computer morphing and gore FX would be mighty tough (and crushingly expensive) to encompass under one roof.

Many studios coming-of-age during the horror boom of the '80s continue to grow, prosper and introduce innovative new techniques to an enthusiastic and wide-eyed audience. Stan Winston toiled on low-budget potboilers like *Dracula's Dog (1977)*, *Mansion of the Doomed (1977)*, *Dead and Buried (1981)*, *Parasite (1982)* and *The Exterminator (1980)* long before hitting paydirt (and an Academy Award or three or four) with *Aliens (1986)*, *Predator (1987)*, *Terminator 2: Judgment Day (1991)*, *Jurassic Park (1993)*, *Interview with the Vampire (1994)*, *The Lost World: Jurassic Park (1997)* and *Jurassic Park III (2001)*. Steve Johnson worked with Rick Baker on *An American Werewolf in London* and *Videodrome* and later formed the prestigious XFX, Inc., creating memorable monsters and mayhem in *Fright Night (1985)*, *Big Trouble in Little China (1986)*, *A Nightmare on Elm Street IV: The Dream Master (1988)*, *The Abyss (1989)* and *Species (1995)*. Howard Berger and Greg Nicotero, apprenticed to Tom Savini during *Day of the Dead (1985)*, worked with Sam Raimi on *Evil Dead 2* and later formed KNB EFX, Inc. with partner Robert Kurtzman. KNB has remained one of the busiest FX studios in Hollywood and their credentials are simply astounding: Craven's *The People Under the Stairs (1991)*, Disney's *Gross Anatomy (1989)*, Kevin Costner's *Dances With Wolves (1990)*, Rob Reiner's *Misery (1990)*, *Bride of Re-Animator (1990)*, *City Slickers (1991)*, Quentin Tarantino's *Reservoir Dogs (1992)*, Carpenter's *In the Mouth of Madness (1995)*,

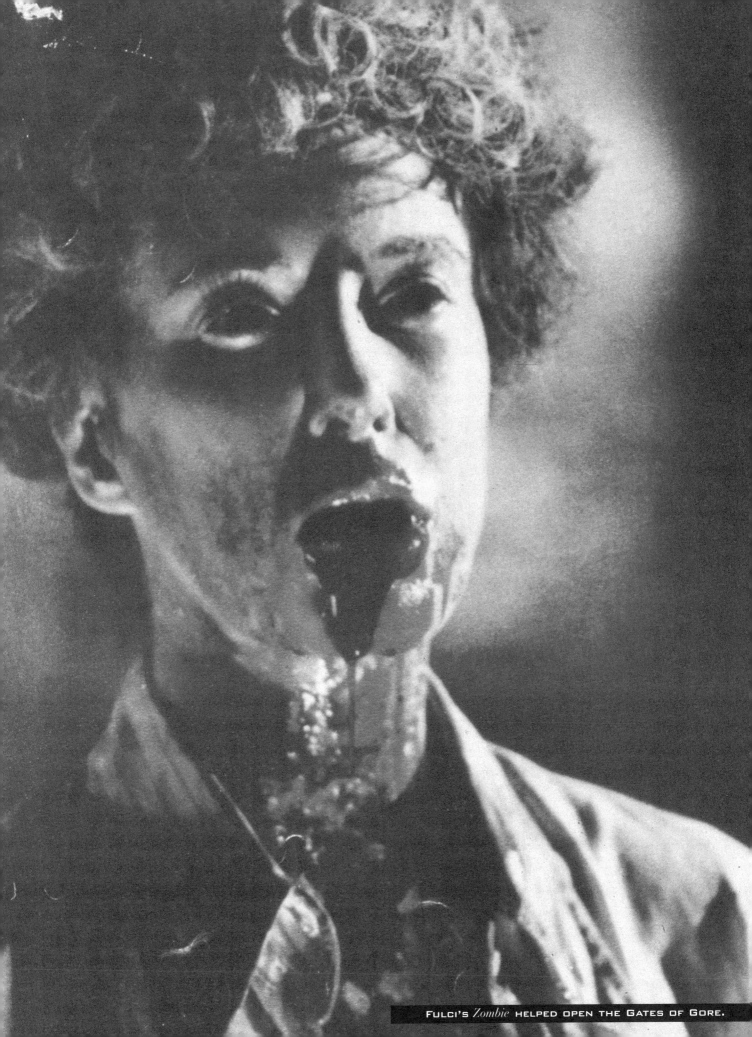

FULCI'S *Zombie* HELPED OPEN THE GATES OF GORE.

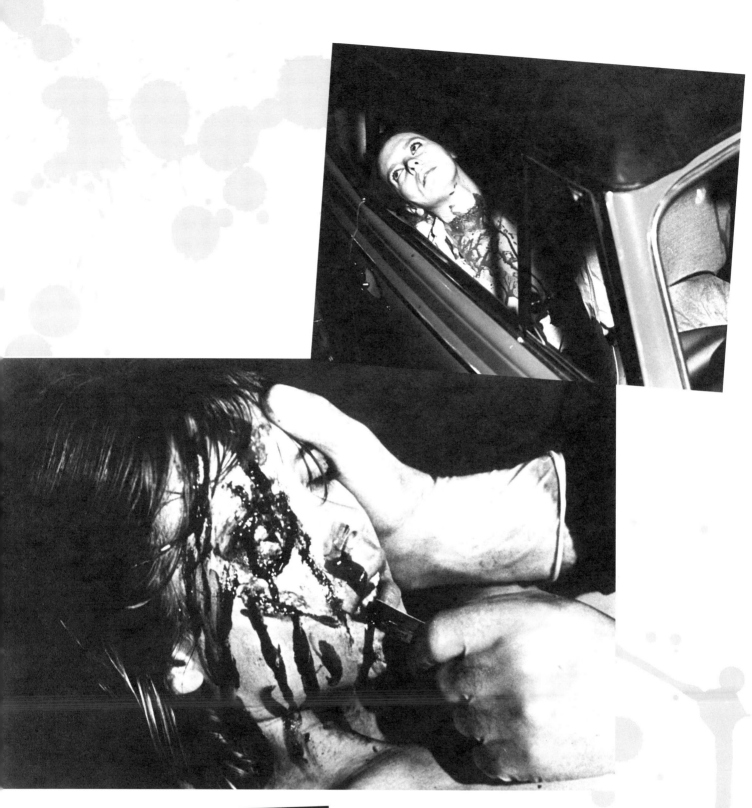

BRUTAL VIOLENCE FROM LUCIO FULCI'S CONTROVERSIAL, EROTIC-SPLATTER OPUS, *The New York Ripper.*

Robert Rodriquez' *From Dusk 'Til Dawn (1996)* and the hi-tech remake of William Castle's *13 Ghosts (2002)* comprise a mere fraction of their output over the last 15 years. KNB also have the dubious distinction of having worked on sequels to four of the longest running horror franchises by contributing major effects to *Friday the 13th: Jason Goes to Hell (1994)*, *Halloween V (1989)*, *A Nightmare on Elm Street V (1989)* and Wes Craven's *New Nightmare (1994)*, and *Leatherface: The Texas Chainsaw Massacre 3 (1990)*. Kurtzman, an avid fan of both Hong Kong action films and director John Woo, made his directorial debut with the futuristic action thriller *The Demolitionist (1996)* for A-Pix Productions. He later helmed *Wishmaster (1997)*, an effects- laden horror/fantasy potboiler written by Clive Barker's ol' pal, Peter Atkins.

While all of these major players remain in heavy demand within the Hollywood splatter circuit, many smaller film studios have had to embrace a major dictum central to the punk rock movement: do it yourself. Jim Muro's *Street Trash*, Jorg Buttgereit's *Nekromantik*, and Peter Jackson's *Bad Taste* and *Dead Alive* are all prime cut chunkblowers that found their wetness within. *Street Trash* (with effects supervised by Jennifer Aspinall) featured a decidely low-tech, but ultra-meaty slate of some of the most outrageous cookie-tossing turmoil ever seen: bodies melting into technicolor pools; decapitation by airborne acetylene tank; severed penis keep-away; full body detonations and enough slime, slop, gore, puke

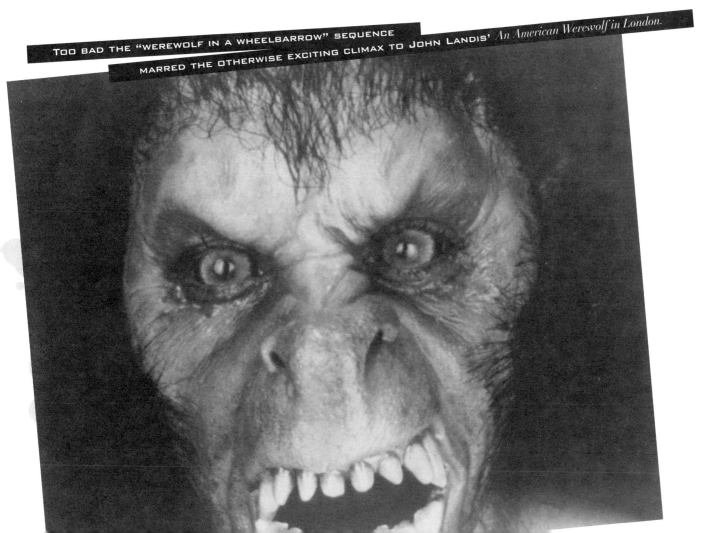

TOO BAD THE "WEREWOLF IN A WHEELBARROW" SEQUENCE MARRED THE OTHERWISE EXCITING CLIMAX TO JOHN LANDIS' *An American Werewolf in London.*

and putrescence to fuel a dozen films. The slow-motion, multi-angled eruption of a 400 pound slimeball who's just guzzled the deadly Tenafly Viper easily proves the poster's boast was no idle threat—"You can't miss us…we're all over the place." *Street Trash* won three European film festivals, including the special Gore Award at Paris Film Fantastique in 1983.

Peter Jackson, actor/director/writer/editor/producer/FX artist, was an unbeatable one-man army in *Bad Taste*. Whether belting in his leaking brains from a cracked cranium or emerging from a gutted, 350 pound alien's ass with a whirring chainsaw, Jackson was indeed, a sight to behold. *Bad Taste* was primo chunkblow material, and what the FX lacked in sophistication and technical expertise, they more than made up for with their wildly anarchic, no-holds-barred panache. Other moist moments to remember and cherish include: multiple dismemberment by axe and chainsaw; numerous heads split and brains splattered; an alien vomit-drinking ritual, and bodies reduced to meat and quivering guts in just under 60 seconds.

When Jackson went into production on *Dead Alive*, he wanted to make a long-delayed homage to his favorite zombie film, *Dawn of the Dead*, but instead he made The Gore Film of the Century. Inarguably the wettest film ever made, *Dead Alive* had horror fans frothing from sea to shining sea. Any film that begins with a splashy, multiple dismemberment by machete before the credits, is obviously seeing red all the way. Besides the usual acts of wanton, interpersonal trauma, we get: pus-spewing; firehose gouts of blood; re-animated spinal columns and twitching, snake-like 40-foot coils of vengeful intestines; maniac babies; babies in blenders; a power mower massacre; kick-ass kung-fu priests; a pair of 160 pound hooters and enough gore to cover the state of Rhode Island to

CLEVER *Halloween* PARODY JUMP-STARTS TOBE HOOPER'S TRIP TO *The Funhouse.*

The Funhouse

a depth of eleven inches. Oh, and there's also a tender, engaging, totally non-cynical love story at the film's core. But by making the World's Wettest Film, Jackson may also have made The Last Gore Film as well. Only the foolish or misguided would attempt a topper. If you don't agree unequivocally, you obviously have not seen the film. But ultimately, it still takes more than gore to shock an audience into submission. Many films pack such an intense, pernicious and lethal sucker-punch to the sensibilities that it's hard to isolate their covert strengths. Many do it on attitude alone. When the Video Revolution unleashed a Pandora's box of Terrors from around the world, aficionados entered a transcendent state of satiation. Now, they could have it all. And easily, too. From shocking sex and splatter bondage atrocities from Asia; to uncut, untamed gutchurners from

European auteaurs like Jean Rollins, Jess Franco, Paul Naschy, Dario Argento, Joe D'Amato and Pier Passolini; South American sauce spectacles from Fauzi Mansur and Coffin Joe (aka Jose Mojica Marins); to hideous, mondo atrocity compilations like *Faces of Death* and *Traces of Death* — it was all as close as your VCR.

Films became available in a variety of formats: NTSC (the American video standard), PAL (the European standard) and import Japanese laser disc. And, best of all, these films were being released in an uncut, unedited form. They were raw, wild, ultra-violent, taboo-trashing anomalies that were potent enough to shock even the most hardened viewer. And they did.

From missing splatter sequences cut from U.S. prints of such films as *Suspiria, Cannibal Holocaust, Phenomena, Breakfast at Manchester Morgue*,

DEMONIC MAYHEM FROM SAM RAIMI'S RELENTLESS *Evil Dead 2: Dead by Dawn*.
THAT'S BROTHER TED AS A POSSESSED CELLAR DWELLER.

MORGAN FREEMAN NEEDS HELP WITH THE SEVEN

DEADLY SINS FROM DAVID FINCHER'S MASTERPIECE OF SUSPENSE, *Seven*.

Pieces, *Cannibal Apocalypse*, *Brain Damage*, *Buried Alive*, *Dawn of the Dead* and *The Beyond*, the gorehound began acquiring a taste for international cuisine and the unfettered and uncensored delights it held.

The video explosion continued to gather momentum, both above and below ground, as collectors bought, sold, traded, pilfered and

with its lurid portrayals of teenagers forced to eat cooked human shit; dine on ground glass hidden in food; be raped repeatedly (both hetero- and homosexual); be pissed and shat upon and be used as human dart boards. Many surmised that Pasolini's early death (shrouded in mystery, but widely accepted as a fatal beating at the hands of a young, gay thug) was somehow related to his

ROB BOTTIN'S REVOLUTIONARY FX WORK IN JOHN CARPENTER'S *The Thing* RAISED THE BAR CONSIDERABLY FOR ONSCREEN MONSTER MAYHEM.

restored films whose controversial contents were causing legal, personal and political repercussions worldwide.

Pier Paolo Passolini's *Salo: The 120 Days of Sodom (1975)*, a perverse and debauched reworking of the infamous tales of the Marquis de Sade updated to a Fascist World War II-era Italy, shocked and repulsed those accustomed to his earlier art-house pieces. And everyone else, too,

dabblings in cinematic debauchery.

Ruggero Deodato's *Cannibal Holocaust* (still not available on commercial U.S. video) was routinely seized, banned and the cause of recurring legal entanglements for its director. Copies of *Nekromantik* were seized in Germany, England, Canada and elsewhere in Europe; many face legal prosecution for its possession. Films like Joe D'Amato's uncut *Grim Reaper (1980)* (aka *Anthropophagus*,

The Savage Island) with its infamous scenes of auto-cannibalism and foetus-eating (actually a skinned rabbit) and *Buried Alive (1981)* (aka *Blue Holocaust, Beyond the Darkness*) with autopsy and crematorium scenes too close for comfort, were banned in Britain and added to an every-growing "Video Nasties" list.

However, it was the Asian connection that was waves generated by a controversial Japanese video series loosely grouped under the *Guinea Pig* moniker.

Supposedly an inspiration for a notorious Japanese copycat killer, the films, especially the highly disturbing "Flower of Flesh and Blood" were once investigated by the FBI as actual "snuff" films. To the trained eye, "Flower of Flesh

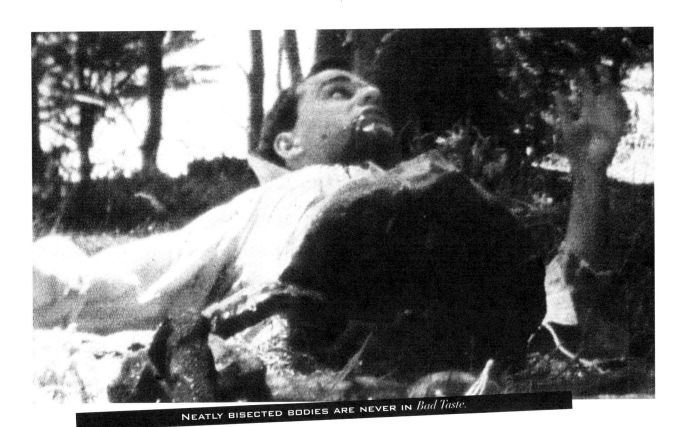

NEATLY BISECTED BODIES ARE NEVER IN *Bad Taste.*

to ultimately prove the most shocking and troubling case of film gone wild. From early Shaw Brother's "X" rated exploitation fare like *Killer Snakes (1979)*, *Black Magic (1980)*, and *The Rape After (1981)* to Tsui Hark's *We're Going to Eat You! (1981)* and the plethora of animal/insect/mondo chunkblowers like *Centipede Horror (1989)*, *Calamity of Snakes (1990)* or *Shocking Asia (1982)*, nothing would compare to the worldwide shock

and Blood" is obvious fakery. There are numerous camera angles employed; professional lighting; slick editing; punched up sound effects and absolutely no nudity. Every single act of violent assault could be easily executed by a journeyman makeup effects artist. This observation was later corroborated by a behind-the-scenes documentary, *The Making of Guinea Pig*, which revealed that the ultra gory torture, dismemberment, beheading

BAD TASTE

with PETER O'HERNE • MIKE MINETT • TERRY POTTER
PETER JACKSON • CRAIG SMITH •

consultant producer TONY HILES
produced and directed by PETER JACKSON

A WINGNUT FILMS PRODUCTION
with support from the
NEW ZEALAND FILM COMMISSION

PETER JACKSON'S DELIGHTFULLY
DEMENTED *Bad Taste,* STARRED
FAT-ASSED, NIXONIAN ALIENS IN
SEARCH OF FRESH MEAT FOR THEIR
INTERGALACTIC BURGER CHAIN.

ALBINO AXE-WHACKERS
ARE WILLING TO SACRIFICE
AN ARM AND A LEG FOR
THEIR ALIEN MASTERS.

and evisceration of a young woman were all accomplished with prosthetics, elementary mechanics, blood tubing and deceptive editing.

Less comforting though, were the revelations made in a book published in 1989 under the title *Unit 731: Japan's Secret Biological Warfare in World War II*, by Peter Williams and David Wallace (first released by Hodder and Stoughton Ltd. in the U.K. and later by The Free Press/MacMillan,Inc. in the U.S.). The book followed on the heels of a vile Chinese series of films which began with *Man Behind the Sun (1988)* and continued through two sequels, *Laboratory of the Devil (1991)* and *Narrow Escape (1993)*. These films deal with an ever-escalating agenda of ghastly and heinous experiments carried out on prisoners of war by an elite Japanese division in a remote village located in occupied Manchuria. Set during the waning days of World War II when a desperate Japan was facing an imminent invasion (or worse) by Allied forces, the film chronicles (in excruciating and lingering detail) a series of medical, biological, and chemical horrors visited upon children, women, old men and imprisoned foreign soldiers. Referred to as "maruta" (or logs of wood), these human guinea pigs were frozen, decompressed, poisoned, autopsied while alive, exposed to various plague viruses and used in ballistics tests by the Japanese Imperial Army. While nearly every single depiction (but not all) of torture was simulated in these films, the impact remains overpowering. More so in the light of the publication of *Unit 731*, which painstakingly documents that nearly all the experiments graphically portrayed in the films has a real-life counterpart. The authors go on to implicate General Douglas MacArthur in

a duplicitous cover-up which spared the real perpetrators in *Unit 731* from facing criminal charges before the War Crimes Tribunal.

Fortunately, most of the ridiculously outrageous splatter films from Asia combine some element of fantasy, adventure, action and twisted humor to make them far more palatable than the grim, malevolent universes explored in *Man Behind The Sun*, *The Rape After (1986)*, *Bloodletters (1986)*, *Flesh and the Bloody Terror (1988)*, *Dr. Lamb (1992)*, *The Unpublished File (1990)* (aka *BBQ Pork Bun, Human Meat Pies*), *Dr. Lamb (1992)*, *Atrocity (1994)*, and *Organ (1996)*. Though no flesh is spared, and bodycounts often grow exponentially amidst geysers of bloody excess, hyper-gore films like *Butterfly and Sword (1993)*, *Savior of the Soul (1992)*, *The Seventh Curse (1986)*, *Black Magic With Buddha (1989)* (aka *Evil Brain*), or *Assassins (1991)* rarely, if ever, cross that line into MondoLand.

In fact, much of the giddy charm of *Story of Ricky (1991)* (aka *Rikki-Oh*), an absolutely insane gore spectacle, is its goofball sense of humor and its cheerful willingness to go over-the-top—time and time again. Though it's a standard issue wronged guy-in-the-slammer scenario, *Story of Ricky* (based on a popular comic book) boasts a charismatic, immensely likeable hero; rambunctious pacing; killer fight scenes; preposterous, but way-cool creatures, and as much gore and fluid spillage as *Bad Taste*. *Story of Ricky* first flirts with gore greatness early-on, during a kick-ass punchfest between our hero and one of the prison's colossally huge, muscle-bound kingpins. Rather than just admit defeat and acknowledge the righteousness of the Way of Ricky, our fallen and battered badass chooses to slice open his own belly and yank his guts out by the bloody handful. Oh, but that's been done. It's when he pulls out a slithering, eight-foot crimson coil of small intestine...and then tries to strangle Ricky with it that the film becomes pure legend. Other prison punks get their eyeballs popped-out; fists punched clean through their torsos; limbs snapped like kindling, or shoved into industrial-strength meat grinders until they're monkey chow.

However, in so many of these Asian splatfests, it's not the gallons of gore, flying limbs or the tubs o' guts that prove troublesome; it's the truly bent, sexually bizarre fetishist angle that's often exploited to the hilt. Sadomasochism, bondage, sodomy, humiliation, dominance, rape and sexual torture seem the only raison de etre for such perverse potboilers as *Entrails of a Virgin (1989)*, *Guts of a Virgin (1990)*, *Robotrix (1991)*, *Rape and Kill (1991)* or *Her Vengeance (1988)*. Many of these freakazoid fuckfests begin to make Joe D'Amato's notorious *Erotic Nights of the Living Dead (1980)* look positively Spielbergian and divinely restrained in contrast.

For many, Hong Kong became the new gore Mecca, as Stateside splat grew leaner and more anemic. Others turned to such diverse foreign sources as Brazil, New Zealand, Australia, Belgium, Germany, Canada or Spain. As a steady

"OH, AND ONE MORE THING, DAN." YOU'RE *dead.*
GARY SHERMAN'S UNDERRATED *Dead and Buried.*

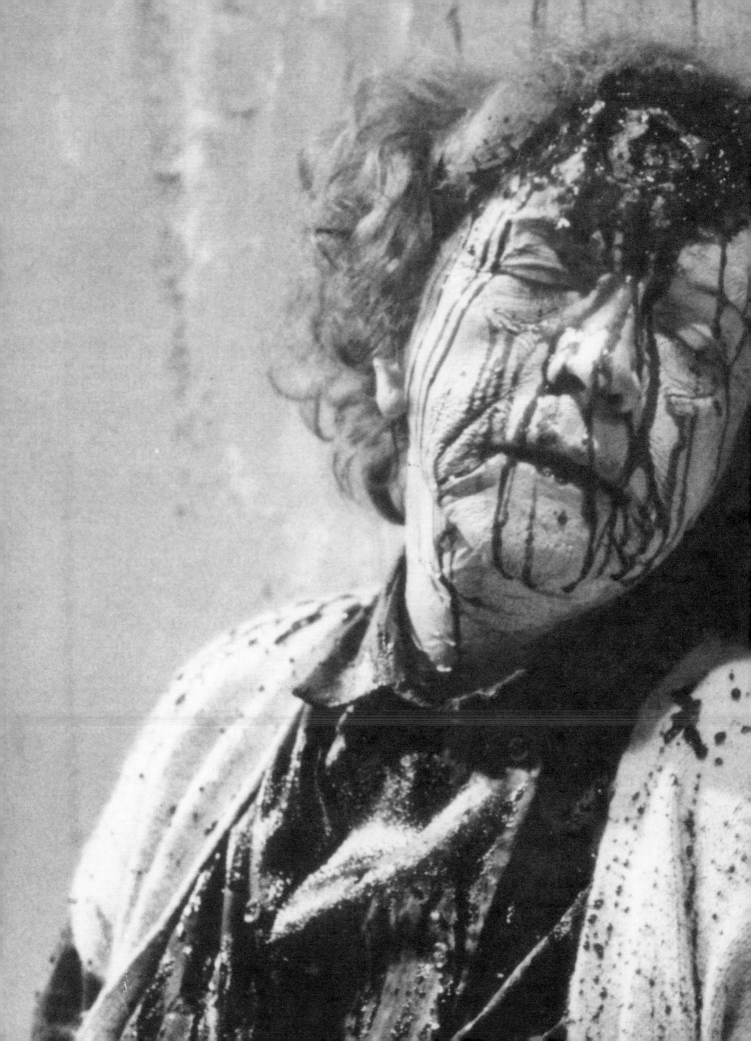

diet of unadulterated splatter was becoming an endangered cuisine, films like Clyde Anderson's ebullient *Zombie 4: After Death (1990)*, Emmanuel Kervyn's *Rabid Grannies (1988)* (uncut festival version only), James A. Martin's *Flesh Eating Mothers (1988)*, Fauzi Mansur's *Ritual of Death (1990)* or *Satanic Attraction (1991)*, or the re-discovered, eclectic wetness of Coffin Joe's *Awakening of the Beast (1968)* and *At Midnight I'll Take Your Soul (1963)* proudly kept the faith.

Not only gore, but the horror film itself appeared in serious decline in the States as the '90s rolled in like a choking fog. Rabid, withering and sustained attacks on violence in film (and violent imagery in popular music) led by newly-annointed media saviors like William Bennet, Cardinal Roger M. Mahoney, Robert Dole, Reverend Robert H. Schuller and Newt Geekrich put the Fear of God in Hollywood. Media conglomerate Time-Warner caved-in when Charlton Heston read the highly incendiary, profane lyrics to Ice-T's bitter "Cop Killer" to a group of horrified and tongue-tied company stockholders. So-called "gangsta rappers" were being held accountable for police killings, drive-by shootings, rapes and drug abuse. Rock & rollers Judas Priest and Ozzy Ozbourne were taking heat (and suffering legal complications) for several teen suicides blamed on their cryptic and gloomy song lyrics. Radio shockjock Howard Stern had to answer over 100 claims of indecency involving his popular program and his employer had to shell out $1.7 million in fines to the Feds.

In 1995, Robert Dole ignited a media firestorm by proclaiming that the violent, horrific, and sexual imagery in films, TV and rap music were "...nightmares of depravity." He also erroneously linked a recent homicide and several other copycat assaults to scenes found in Woody Harrelson and Wesley Snipes' buddy-pic, *Money Train (1995)*. When confronted with evidence to the contrary (none of the perpetrators had even seen the film), Dole was smugly, unabashedly unrepentant. "I make no apologies for speaking out on the excesses of the entertainment industry. Non-stop images of ever more graphic and senseless violence debase our culture and affect the attitudes and conduct of our impressionable young."

Over 50 years ago, in his seminal novel *1984*, George Orwell feared a future society where "Ignorance is Strength" and "Freedom is Slavery."

In 1987, Clive Barker asserted, "There are no limits."

Now, in this Brave New World, it's your call, Bunky.

It is Evil Beyond Time and Imagination...

Forever Watching... Waiting... Killing!

Forever Evil

Starring

Red Mitchell   **Tracey Huffman**   **Charles Trotter**   **Howard Jacobsen**

Directed by **Roger Evans**   Produced by **Jill Clark**   Screenplay by **Freeman Williams**

Music by **Marianne Pendino**   Photography by **Horacio Fernandez**

VHS hi-fi STEREO   Beta hi-fi STEREO

WARNING: Not for the squeamish!
Explicit violence and gore. Don't see it alone.

UNITED
HOME VIDEO

©1987 United Entertainment, Inc.
PRINTED IN U.S.A.

thE goOd, ThE bAd anD the BLoOdy

Buried Treasures? *Hardly*. They might have been buried somewhat, agreed, but you'll find precious few, real, honest-to-shit treasures here. But that's not really the point here now, is it? Some films, like most dogs, enter the portals of our hearts through other means, seemingly unrelated to their breeding, appearance, behavior or scent. A stinky, unwanted junkyard mutt can become a Man's Best Friend. A funky-assed flick that everyone else thinks blows can be your comfort in times of pretense, posturing and over-produced, witless genre droppings that are obscenely expensive, pedigreed and supposedly housebroken. And, some films are just so clueless, so truly fucked-up that you feel really shitty delivering further kicks to the ribs. Maybe some films fail gracelessly, indeed, but somewhere, deep down, you know they were really trying to be good dogs. Most, though, just tried to make a quick, easy buck on their way to somewhere else; but at least

they were honest about it. Any time a film promises to show a "...Man Turned Inside Out!," or it "Guarantees to Upset Your Stomach!," or provides a $5,000 insurance policy for "Death by Fright," you know the filmmakers are winking with their fingers crossed. But, often, the hucksterism, the brash and unfulfillable boasts, and the spit-in-your-eye attitude provide a welcome relief to a hemorraghing, big-budgeted studio misfire that promises much and delivers mulch.

Sometimes a dinky, hardscrabble budget forces filmmakers to be far more bold, clever and experimental and frees them from the normal conventions of commercial filmmaking. But, then again, lots of these projects are out-of-focus, ploddingly inane, and void of any apparent talent either in front of or behind the camera. It's always a crapshoot, pards. Fortunately, with the abundance of information now available in film magazines, on the Internet, on special release DVDs,

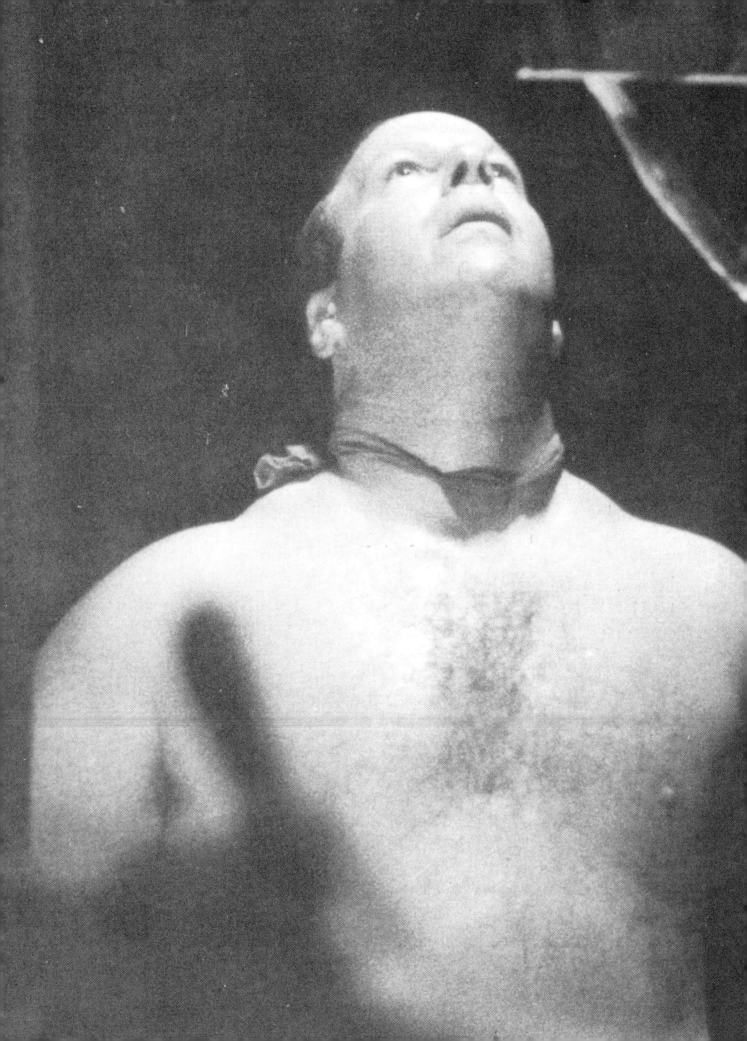

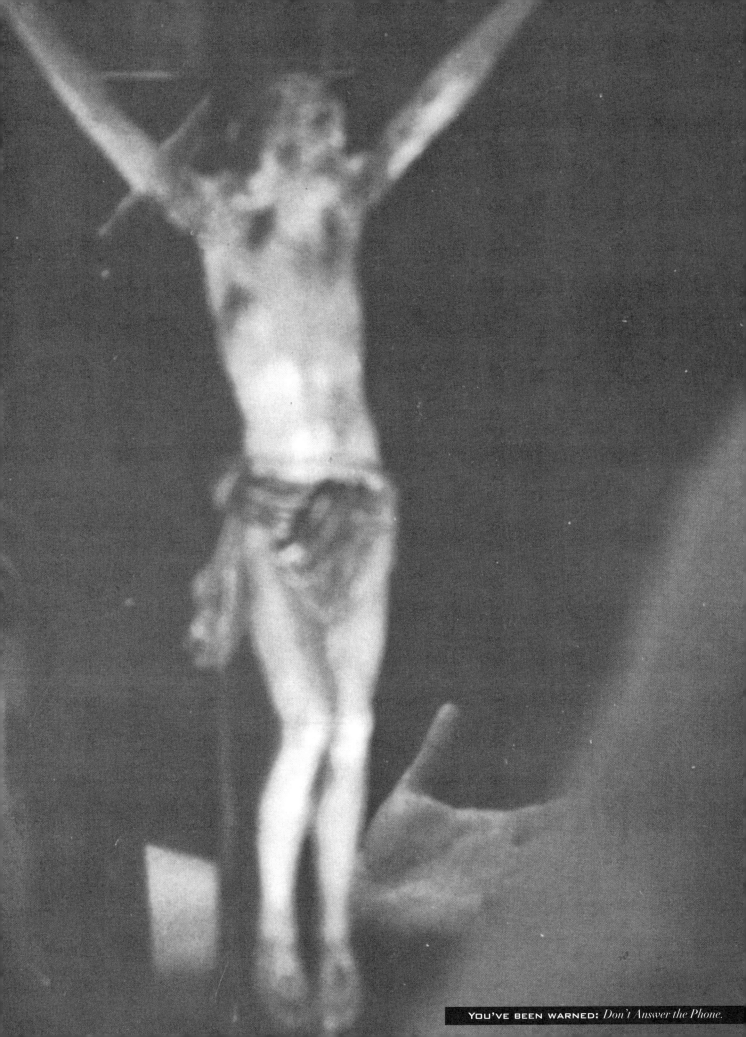

YOU'VE BEEN WARNED: *Don't Answer the Phone.*

and in the fan press, your chances of finding some real "buried treasure" increase to about 1-in-25. And those are pretty good odds, bunky.

By now, it seems as though nearly every image shot through a motion picture camera has turned up on videotape, laser disc, DVD, cable special or CD-Rom. There remains a raft of films that just never gained entry into the popular lexicon of the devoted sleazophile. Few of these films are really "lost" and all are available in one format or another. But if one gauges their worth by the amount of ink or word-of-mouth they've generated, they're practically flat-lining. Many prints are lost, destroyed or simply forgotten when companies fail, merge or reduce their old inventories. Some suffer from copyright and legal entanglements, others from regional distribution problems. And, of course, some are just so shitty that only an unrepentant gorehound with terminal common sense issues can ever embrace them.

To many aficionados of the wet, the wild, the really weird, there will never be enough films about airborne piranhas; zoo animals on angel dust; 9-foot cockroach-humanoids; toxic, metastasizing abortions; flesh-eating mothers; rabid grannies; 18-inch Ratboys; or 385 lb. homicidal butchers in love with a pig. No, sir, no way.

Often, through no apparent intent on the filmmaker's part, a movie accidentally stumbles upon a formula that will be knocked-off, endlessly repeated, sequelized, and reinvented—eventually becoming a sub-genre in and of itself.

Guerdon Trueblood's surprisingly effective and unsettling *The Candy Snatchers (1973)* was a creepy detour into edgy, reality-based horror echoing similar themes found in such hardcore films as *Last House on the Left (1972)*, *The Texas Chainsaw Massacre (1974)*, or *House on the Edge of the Park (1980)*. When kidnappers snatch Candy off the streets and bury her alive, they begin a war of wits with both her wealthy parents and among themselves as a series of diabolic plot twists sends the film into ever-darkening cycles of despair. Though the film addresses and eventually tiptoes around such controversial plot devices as rape, incest, murder, dope and dismemberment, *The Candy Snatchers* is a remarkably taut, well-directed and accomplished creepfest.

When the Canadian thriller *Black Christmas (1974)* premiered, few would have predicted the film's lingering impact on the next decade's thrillers. Predating John Carpenter's *Halloween (1978)* and such lesser efforts as *When a Stranger Calls (1979)* and *Don't Answer the Phone (1980)*, Bob (*Deathdream*) Clark's superior thriller deftly establishes both the killer-in-the-house subgenre as well as the maniac-on-the-phone scenario. The film's tight, no-nonsense style slowly ratchets up the suspense until a clever twist (for its time) at the climax provides a nice coda. Also released as *Stranger in the House* and *Silent Night, Evil Night*, Clark's film also boasts of an unusually protean cast including Margot (*Superman*) Kidder, Olivia (*Romeo & Juliet*) Hussey, Keir (*2001: A Space Odyssey*) Dullea, Andrea (*Second City TV*) Martin and genre workhorse John (*Cannibal Apocalypse, Nightmare on Elm Street*) Saxon.

Mansion of the Doomed (1975) (aka *The Eyes of Dr. Cheney, Massacre Mansion*) was produced by a then 21-year-old entrepreneur by the name of Charles Band, who would later become the head cheese at both Empire Pictures and Full Moon

Pictures, producing hundreds of crap-ass titles that make *Mansion* look like *The Magnificent Ambersons*. Although the film earns Hollywood has-beens Richard Basehart and Gloria Grahame some much-needed pocket change, it also provided work for budding genre personalities Lance (*Aliens*) Henriksen and multi-Academy Award-winning FX artist Stan Winston, who designed the graphic, gory makeups. The film is sleazy and cheap, but somewhat effective in spite of itself, as Basehart's Dr. Cheney begins a series of hasty eye transplantations in hopes of restoring his daughter's eyesight. The ham-fisted attempts at black comedy occasionally work and Winston's freaky, eye-less makeups are genuinely creepy, making this somewhat clumsy updating of George Franju's classic *Les Veux sans Visage (1959)* (aka *Eyes Without a Face, Horror Chamber of Dr. Faustus*) marginally watchable.

The sex, gore and death-by-garden-tool subgenre would get an early start with both Niko Mastorakis' *Island of Death (1975)* (aka *Island of Perversion*) and David Paulsen's *The Savage Weekend (1976)*. *Island of Death* is an unpleasant, desperately naughty cavalcade of escalating debauchery that wallows happily in graphic gore, nudity, sex, incest, voyeurism, bestiality, gay-bashing, proliferate pissing and carnal carnage, all to surprisingly little effect. Besides the usual deaths by handgun, knives, nails and spears, the film also boasts of perhaps the first and only on-screen decapitation-by-bulldozer. It all sounds way, way better than it really plays.

The Savage Weekend (aka *The Upstate Murders, Killer Behind the Mask*) employs the masked killer-with-an-arsenal-of-power-tools formula to little or no effect, summarily wasting the talents of David (*Re-Animator*) Gale and William (*Blade Runner*) Sanderson. The rampant, gratuitous nudity proves a welcome relief and Caitlin O' Heany's boner-inducing choice of sleazy lingerie remains the film's high point.

BEASTS GREAT and SMALL

Many films succeed or fail on the strength of their special effects—especially those that have precious little to offer in the way of plot, characters, direction or pacing. Some films succeed in spite of themselves—their bargain basement monsters proudly shown without apology—and endear themselves to cynical audiences used to ferreting out the blue screen shots, CGI effects, prosthetic seams and cutaways at a nanosecond's notice. It's easy to see why low budget, independent filmmakers in the '70s and '80s chose the slasher/stalker/serial killer route; it was cheap, audience-friendly and didn't have to rely on elaborate makeup FX, prosthetics, armatures, animation or puppetry. Plenty of aspiring genre hotshots, however, threw caution to the winds and either fearlessly or foolishly, filled their flicks with horndog mutant apes; terminator pigs; cranky crocs; buzz-bombing piranhas; deformed ambulatory abortions; giant cockroach queens and tiny, rat-like monstrosities conceived by an unholy pairing of monkey spunk and rodent ovum. Besides, seeing a highly agitated, chattering, airborne piranha expertly negotiate a hotel's hallways in search of fresh meat is a cinematic scenario not likely to be repeated again in our lifetime. And, when would you expect a freshly-

STEVEN SPIELBERG CALLED JOE DANTE'S *Piranha* THE ALL-TIME BEST *Jaws* RIP-OFF.

flushed, aborted fetus to be reborn as a giant toxic slopsack that just wants to crawl back home and park in mommy's garage? Even when many of these films fall flat on their incompetent little asses, you can't help but note the moxie, the madness, the metastasizing mind-melting going on behind the camera lens.

However, as movie audiences became more accustomed to elaborate effects, animatronics, and computer-enhanced imagery, many films were summarily shunned for their crummy, amateurish effects work and the patently phony creatures they summoned. And now, even shit-brained, low budget yawners boast credible CGI effects, complicated makeups, extensive anima-

tronics and a plethora of inventive sight gags. The cheeseball monster flick may be gone, perhaps, but most assuredly, not forgotten.

In light of his current and well-sustained career meltdown arc, Tobe Hooper's *Eaten Alive (1976)* (aka *Death Trap*, *Starlight Slaughter*) now appears, arguably, as a "near masterpiece." Eschewing the harsh, in-your-face, documentary-style of *The Texas Chainsaw Massacre*, Hooper serves up a stylized, patently phony *mis-en-scene*; garish lighting; outlandish performances; and one piss-poor, anemic alligator. Most of it works, but only fitfully. One thing for sure, though, Neville Brand is a fuckin' four-star hoot as the one-legged, scythe-wielding wack job operating a run-

ROB BOTTIN'S *Piranha* FX WERE CLEVERLY SHOT TO DISGUISE THE FACT THAT THEY HAD LESS THAN A DOZEN OF THE TOOTHY TERRORS TO WORK WITH.

down hotel in the Louisiana swamps who feeds unwanted guests to his pet alligator. Marilyn Burns proves once again she's the real and original Queen of the Scream, and both Carolyn Jones (Morticia on TV's *Addams Family*) and family patriarch Mel Ferrer demonstrate the dead can, indeed, still walk...and act when provoked. William Finley (who returns in Hooper's *The Funhouse*) as a henpecked suburban nerd is nearly as looney tunes as Brand, but suffers an ignominious demise between a nasty blade and an even nastier bite. In a brief, but memorable pre-Freddy Krueger role, Robert Englund's character introduces himself as "I'm Buck—and I love to fuck!" *Eaten Alive* also distinguishes itself with a pretty

cool poster and a splendidly sleazy tagline (later nicked by *Shogun Assassin*): "Meet the maniac and his friend. Together they make the greatest team in the history of mass slaughter." Kinda makes ya tingle a bit, no?

Alfred Sole, director of the cult classic *Alice, Sweet Alice* (1977) (aka *Communion*, *Holy Terror*), gets lost in the jungle (well, Puerto Rico actually) with *Tanya's Island* (1980), a lushly photographed, schizoid souffle of pretentious arthouse banter; thinly veiled bestiality; rampant nudity; and creature carnage. D.D. Winters, who later became "Vanity" and an intimate Prince Pal, is a hot babe married to a bipolarized macho painter who begins resenting his wife's dalliances with the island's wildlife. She fantasizes about "Blue," a sensitive, humanoid ape and is soon struck by a severe case of hot monkey love. It all leads to a coconut-tossing confrontation and much heavy speculation about the nature of man and the time-space continuum. Winters is nearly naked most of the time and the realistic and effective apesuit was designed by young creature connoisseurs Rick Baker and Rob Bottin.

It's not difficult to trace the source of inspiration for Italian workhorse Enzo G. Castellari's *The Last Shark (1981)* (aka *Great White*). The film's missing-in-action status was precipitated by both Steven Spielberg and Universal Studios' successful copyright infringement lawsuit, which effectively rendered the film dead in the water. And no wonder, *The Last Shark* is lifted nearly intact from the *Jaws (1977)* template, with James Franciscus playing an amalgam of the Roy Scheider and Richard Dreyfuss characters while Vic Morrow's blustery old salt is a xerox copy of the Robert Shaw role. For years, rumors persisted that a stunt man was actually eaten alive during filming, though scant evidence exists of such an encounter in the finished print. The mechanical shark blows squid dick, but the stock footage of several great whites in full feeding frenzy fervor remains butt-clenchingly effective and suitably hair-raising. Several poorly made dummies get bitten in half; a 12" plastic toy helicopter crashes in a bathtub; and a breakaway pier carries a couple dozen terrified tourists off to appetizer land. It's actually modestly entertaining, well-produced and much better than you'd ever think.

A long time ago, in a Caribbean jungle far, far away, the director of *The Terminator (1984)*, *Aliens*

(1986) and *Titanic (1995)* was paying some early dues. The U.S/Italian co-production of *Piranha II:The Spawning (1981)*(aka *The Flying Killers*) featured a mutant hybrid of piranha and flying fish hatched during secret biological experiments by a quasi-military cadre of borderline loonies. A hasty suspension of disbelief is *de rigeur* for the crowd scenes involving flying killer puppets emerging from the surf and chasing *los touristas* down the halls of their beachside resort, and it plays just about as stupid as it sounds. A sequel in name only to Joe Dante's superlative *Piranha (1978)*, James Cameron's inauspicious genre debut showed little, if any, of the ambitious directorial flair he would soon develop. *Piranha II* also featured Lance Henriksen, who would later rejoin the Cameron Crew on *Aliens*. The not-so-special effects were by Gianetto (*Zombie*) de Rossi and in a sly nod to the chestburster scene in *Alien (1979)*, one of the toothy tormentors bloodily erupts from the torso of one unfortunate party dog. Cameron was reportedly fired before production was completed and *Piranha II* has never made an appearance on the "King of the World's" Hollywood resume. Methinks he got even in due time.

Rampaging zoo animals, high on angel dust, take center stage in Franco Prosperi's refreshingly ridiculous *The Wild Beasts (1983)*. When PCP is accidentally (wha?) dropped into a German zoo's water supply, the cheetahs, polar bears, elephants and pigs start a rumble; they're quickly joined by assorted rats, guide dogs and kitty cats, all high as kites and looking for trouble. An unruly mob of ripped-to-the-whiskers rodents attack a lovesick couple and chew their faces off while a righteously stoned pachyderm stands on a little girl's head and

THE BEASTLY BOGOSITY THAT SINKS THE FEEBLE *Shriek of the Mutilated.*

Shriek of the Mutilated.

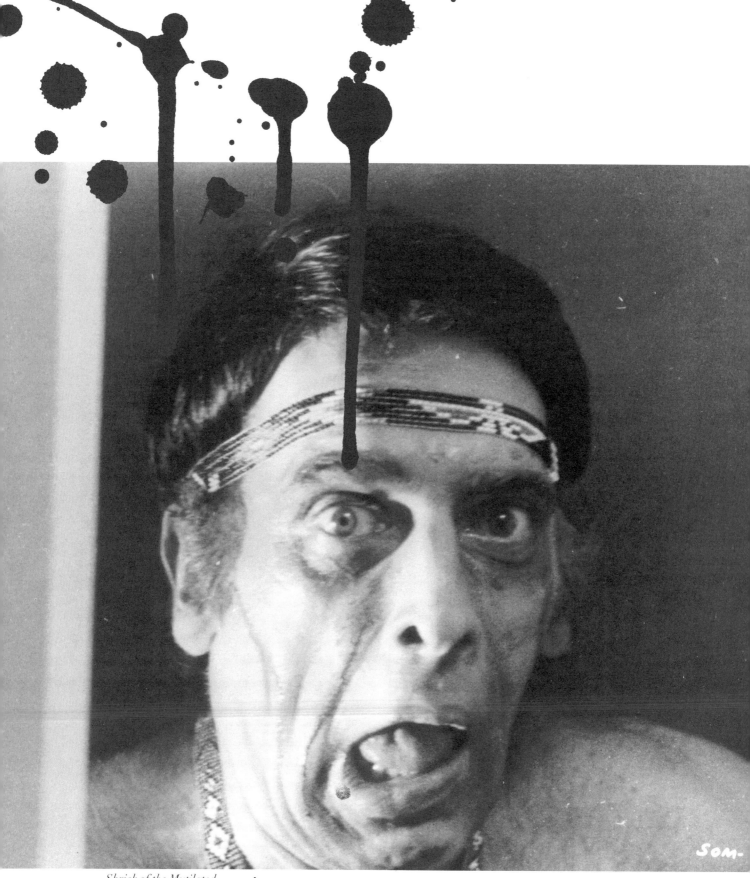

Shriek of the Mutilated WASN'T EVEN AS SCARY AS THIS LOBSTER'S HEADBAND.

turns her cabeza into a nutty, crunchy jello salad. Director Prosperi, clearly well-past his career peak but still trying gamely, was behind such controversial shockumentaries as *Mondo Cane (1961)* and *Africa Addio (1966)* (retitled by schlockmeister Jerry Gross as *Africa: Blood and Guts*).

Rowdy rodents, rabbits, grasshoppers, ants, bees, bears, dogs and other assorted quadripeds, reptiles and invertebrates have always figured into genre offerings; but the undisputed Grand Whole Hog of Colossal Porcine Splatter remains Russel Mulcahy's *Razorback (1984)*. Set in the Australian Outback and gorgeously photographed by Dean Semler, the film provides Mulcahy with plenty of opportunity to showcase his flashy directorial style honed by years of work on commercials and music videos. *Razorback* is a haunting, surreal, frequently inspired creature feature that makes terrific (if somewhat limited) use of its awesome, tank-sized King Pig, designed and built by Bob McCarron. Even more unsettling is the sublimely creepy slaughterhouse sets, where kangaroo killers, running a clandestine dog food factory, form an unholy alliance with the Supreme Squealer. Mulcahy later went on to more mainstream fare including *Highlander (1986)* and its sequel, as well as *The Shadow (1994)*.

Employing real human freaks as screen monsters has always been a risky road to take; and even if the film succeeds somewhat, it still tends to leave a bad taste in one's mouth. That said, Guiliano Carnimeo's *Ratman (1987)* is a diverting bit of PastaLand sideshow perversity that stars "The World's Smallest Man," the 27-inch tall Dominican Republic runt, Nelson de la Rosa. The titular character comes into being as the result of

a god-knows-what-the-fuck kind of unholy experiment involving rat sperm and monkey pussy. An identity-bending, intra-species rodent rampage follows shortly, as our little ratscal indulges his newly discovered Super Ratastic powers with an applaudable gusto. The sets are cheap, the flick's dark and grainy, but there's plenty of cool, unselfconscious gore and passable star turns by Fulci vets Janet (*City of the Living Dead*) Agren and David (*The Beyond*) Warbeck.

Though killer croc and aggro-alligator creature features are nothing new, a nifty spin was put on *Dark Age (1987)*, an Australian potboiler that stars a 25-foot mythic crocodile god; an adoring aboriginal croc cult; breathtaking scenery; and enough gung-ho camera pyrotechnics to make your head spin right off your spine. The cult leader is essayed by David Gulpillil, a deep-dish, dark chocolate, butt-ugly native actor who's apparently required by law to appear in every single film shot Down Under (*Walkabout*, *The Last Wave*, etc.). Though this plays much like a version of *Jaws in Queensland*, the acting is solid and believable; with top drawer production values; and a serviceable, effective mechanical crocodile that easily gulps a baby down in one staggering bite.

Though schlockmeister William Castle introduced us to gigantic, hissing pyrotechnic cockroaches that could spell in *Bug (1975)* and George Romero toyed with the cockroach as carnivore in a *Creepshow (1982)* segment, the world remained unprepared for the glorious, mutant insectoid chunkblowing panache of *The Nest (1987)*. Since these genetically engineered roach hybrids become what they eat, we get a delightful assortment of animal and human cockroach combos that are bound to please even the most discerning aficionado of the Insect Fear subgenre. Robert Lansing, a veteran of other big bug blowouts like *Empire of the Ants (1977)*, is a corrupt, small town mayor of an island resort trying to protect his interests from an ever-multiplying army of clever, task-sharing, super roaches whose queen is nine feet tall and plenty pissed off. Lansing loses the battle and quickly mutates into a slimy, multi-appendaged RoachMan who tries to eat his own daughter. There is a fine turn by Terri Treas as a foxy scientist who is sexually aroused by roach bites and a funky restaurant rampage set to the beat of "La Cucaracha." A wise, homily-spouting existential exterminator named Homer keeps things in perspective. This Roach Romp Rocks! Trust me.

Any film that commences with a solemn warning about the unspeakable horrors that befell a cursed, illegal abortion clinic then stridently suggests that the audience immediately employ their "Suckling Prevention Kit," is wearing its heart (and guts) right there on its sleeve. Frances Teri's *The Suckling (1989)* is a splendid, off-color, tasteless mess that is unapologetically gory, kinky and terminally twisted. After an aborted fetus is flushed down the clinic's toilet, it splashes down in some virulent toxic waste and begins its metamorphosis into a large, slobbering slime beast that misses his mommy. In one of its more audacious, chunkblowing moments of inspired mayhem, the adult-stage, mutated ambulatory abortion makes a heart-rending attempt to crawl back into Mom's oven and become born again. With plenty of deep-dish black humor, funky sex romps and gore to go, *The Suckling* proves once again that Bad

Taste is truly timeless. Michael Gingold, now an editor at *Fangoria* magazine, took a turn inside the snarky slime suit—much to his eternal credit.

Many films eschew the monster/creature angle in favor of focusing on the most dangerous animal on the face of the earth: man. It's a lot cheaper too—no complicated makeups, prosthetics, animatronics or technological snafus on set—to go *mano a mano*. Man's unrequited black heart of darkness has long been the source for many of the bleakest, most truly disturbing films ever made. So instead of relying on special effects and elaborate *mis-en-scenes*, many directors simply let the cast run a bit wild—all in the service of the plot, of course. For some of these wild and wooly renegades, it's a wonder they were ever made, let alone released to totally unsuspecting audiences.

Distributed by exploitation maestro William Mishkin under such titles as *Staying Alive*, *Held Hostage* and *Bloodbath at 1313 Fury Drive*, Robert A. Endelson's *Fight for Your Life (1977)* is such a virulent, racist, inciteful potboiler that its chances of surviving our current politically correct climate would be far less than nil. Because of the numerous titles the film was released under, it was often confused with other exploitation flicks with lurid titles. Also distributed as *I Hate Your Guts*, Endelson's film was sometimes confused with an early Roger Corman racial melodrama by the same name that was also released as *The Intruder (1961)*. Corman's film starred William Shatner in a highly controversial role as a black-baiting, Southern racist; but both films are so far apart in intent and execution, only a real rube would be misled by the shared title. *Fight for Your Life* stars the ever-reliable character actor William Sanderson, who would also appear in Ridley Scott's *Blade Runner* (1982) and become a regular on *The Bob Newhart Show* on network TV. Sanderson is a hardass convict who leads a bloody escape from prison along with both a Mexican and Chinese con, who eventually hole-up with a black minister's family. This eclectic racial stew allows the filmmakers a broad canvas upon which to splash a furious, ear-stinging assortment of racist epithets simply unparalleled in contemporary cinema. No stone is left unturned, except maybe the one used to bash a youngster's brains out in a tender, loving closeup. No matter what the title, *Fight for Your Life* is a bruising, hateful, prickly film that will stay with you for years.

A very effective and wicked spin on the *Death Wish* formula is exploited expertly in both *The Exterminator* (1980) and its rollicking sequel, *Exterminator II* (1984). Both films star Robert Ginty as a Vietnam vet with major vigilante issues on his agenda and the hardware to back up his boasts. One of his favorite tools for cleaning up the streets is a flamethrower, so the ante (and body count) is raised considerably in the sequel when Ginty goes gonzo aboard an armor-plated, flame-spewing garbage truck. Loads of cool stunts, crunching car crashes and flashy explosions only sweeten the lethal mix. According to Leonard Maltin's *Movie and Video Guide*, which rated both films as "bombs," the sequel is "Obnoxious, grade-Z garbage." So, who ya gonna trust here, bunky?

Roberta Findlay, half of the husband and wife team responsible for such cinematic bogosities as *Shriek of the Mutilated* (1974), *Snuff* (1974), and a handful of shitty porno films, delivers a none-too-

subtle kick in the balls with the brutal, frequently hair-raising actioner, *Tenement* (1985) (aka *Game of Survival*). This gritty, ultraviolent urban assault flick pits a multi-ethnic gang of Bronx street toughs against the elderly residents of a downtown fleabag hotel, who are not quite as helpless as they first appear. The violence and aberrant anti-social behavior grows increasingly ugly: eyes are gouged with scissors; blades slid into nutsacks; and broomsticks shoved into orifices they have no business being in. Wicked electrocutions, impalements and razor rampages add further sauce to this simmering stew. *Tenement* is well-paced, suspenseful and, at times, excruciating to witness. Findlay's only other claim to fame came at a very high price — her husband was decapitated by a helicopter rotor blade atop a New York skyscraper while scouting for film locations.

If the cast and credits of Josh Becker's *Thou Shalt Not Kill...Except* (1985) (aka *Stryker's War*) look familiar, they should — many of Becker's buddies were major players in the *Evil Dead* films. Sam Raimi and brother Ted headline while Scott Spiegel (writer/producer) and Bruce Campbell (co-writer) assume roles on the camera's other side. Shot for around $250,000 in and around Detroit, the film posits the question: "What if Rambo met Charles Manson?" The answer here is obvious: a hefty body count punctuated by hyper-violent gunplay; punji-stick impalements; lacerated flesh; Vietnam flashbacks and mucho macho male-bonding stuff. Raimi plays a rabid cult leader with really shitty teeth and an equally culpable fright wig, who kidnaps babies, tortures senior citizens and barbecues cute little doggies. He makes a fatal mistake kidnapping the wife of a recently returned Vietnam vet and pays dearly for it in a deliciously staged sequence of divine exsanguination. Becker went on to direct Ted Raimi in a starring role in *Lunatics: A Love Story (1992)*, a deliberately offbeat, goofball comedy romance co-starring Deborah Foreman and (of course) Bruce Campbell.

Oftimes, in order to secure a more user-friendly "R" (Restricted) or PG-13 rating from the lobsters at the MPAA, films undergo a radical metamorphosis; lose minutes of footage; get a new title and emerge all the worse for wear. Some films scissor out most of the blood and gore, drop some of the cheesier moments, and desperately try to squeak by on cinematic merit alone. Most fail. Eviscerating an exploitation film's guts usually renders it unpalatable to both mainstream and cult audiences. And, some films are saddled with such crappy and misleading titles that it's difficult to ascertain just what market they were really aiming for. Other films slither by only because they showcase a handful of totally outrageous, barf-bagging mayhem that almost justifies the film's very existence.

Roger Evan's *Forever Evil (1987)* is an unconscionably bloated, 107-minute test of endurance, but, fortunately, contains a few sequences of knockout grossness sure to please the beast in all of us. Uneasily mixing elements of such diverse fare as *The Big Chill (1983)* and *The Evil Dead*; adding a bit of fourth-rate Lovecraftian demonology; and then tossing in way too many supporting players, *Forever Evil* still manages several showstopping moments of pure chunkblowing genius. When an otherwordly demon (That's Yog Kathog to you, pardner), summoned by an arcane ritual crashes their chillin' party, yuppie splat soon hits the fan in any number of colorful, inventive and super chunky examples of extreme exsanguination. The real topper arrives when a

Rabid Grannies IS ALL WET...BUT ONLY IN THE "UNRATED" VERSION.

possessed young woman graphically performs a late term self-abortion, ripping her demon child from her dripping womb in a shower of red and righteous gruel. One of the still photos of the nude, gutted, mommy-to-be lying splayed on the bathroom floor was, in fact, the one and *only* photo ever pulled from print by the former publisher of your reporter's own *Deep Red* magazine.

The opening credits of Rick Roessler's *Slaughterhouse (1987)* offers a pig's-eye view of a nasty, *Faces of Death*-style sequence inside a real meat processing plant set to a jaunty, bouncing musical number that readily betrays what's really happening on screen. It's an unsettling opening to be sure, one of many cleverly inspired bits in a film that attempts to blend hair-raising violence with crafty black humor a la *The Texas Chainsaw Massacre*. It doesn't always work, but Roessler displays some accomplished camera work, atmospheric set pieces and several well-defined, achingly eccentric characters. Lester Bacon and his man-mountain son Buddy are facing foreclosure on their decrepit pig farm just as some teen twitoids are in the process of shooting a horror video on the premises. That sets the stage for an eclectic body count of county inspectors, cops and rutting juveniles—messily dispatched by cleaver, mallet and assorted porker paraphernalia by a towering, snorting and squealing Buddy, nicely essayed by Big Joe Barton. Buddy's also in love with his prize porcine pal, precipitating numerous tender and romantic moments between sow and psycho. The hulking, 385-pound Barton could easily go toe-to toe with the original Leatherface (Gunnar Hansen) and not be found wanting. Lots o'funky music too, white boy, in a film that's way better than you'd think. Seek out the rare, uncut director's print for maximum moistness.

By all means, avoid at all costs the trimmed down "R"-rated versions of both Emmanuel

MORE *Granny* GORE...

Kervyn's *Rabid Grannies (1988)* and James A. Martin's *Flesh Eating Mothers (1988)*. When the dreaded Troma Team got a hold of *Rabid Grannies*, which had already won some European FX awards, they cut nearly all the gore, kept the lame-ass comedy, and delivered an undigestible, unfunny bit of cinematic swill that everyone hated. The first half of the film is slow, talky and relatively pointless; but by the last few reels, things get red, wet and wild in a hurry. During a combo birthday bash and family reunion at an isolated mansion, a mysterious package arrives from one of the celebrant's Satanically-inclined younger family members. The drinks get spiked and before you can say *Demons for a Day*, the birthday gals turn into metamorphosing, malevolent harpies who unleash the Red Tide in a variety of colorful and extreme exercises in righteous chunkblowing. The saucy impalements; multiple dismemberments; cannibalism and gut-yankings frequently spray the screen with firehose gouts of blood that only a real party pooper wouldn't love. Be sure to seek out the "director's uncut festival print." The "R"-rated Troma version should come equipped with an auto-erase function.

A kind of *Stepford Wives* meets *Cannibal Apocalypse* pastiche, James Martin's *Flesh Eating Mothers* is a semi-hip, gore comedy nearly flat-lined by inert direction and pedestrian musical accompaniment; but, nonetheless, the sauce is the story here. When a sexually transmitted virus infects the Super Soccer Moms of a pleasant suburban wasteland, several new cuts of meat begin to make an appearance on numerous nuclear family unit's dining tables. These now-voracious, predatory mothers supplement their family's menus with prime cuts of little babies, Little Leaguers, curious cops and philandering husbands. It's witty and wet—nicely summed up by a kid who's just murdered his mommy: "Hey, I had to shoot her! She would've eaten me too!"

Though Carlton J. Albright's *Luther the Geek (1989)* earned a modest buzz in the underground market, spotty distribution and lackluster promotion prevented the film from really connecting with its intended audience. The film is one of very few attempts to address the real "geek" issue; it's no ordinary nerd, bro,' but a carnival sideshow freak who bites the heads off live animals, usually chickens. When little Luther witnesses a real geek in action, shown in a compelling, truly disarming prologue, he accidentally gets his teeth knocked out and is then further humiliated by a jeering mob. They will pay, of course—and oh, how they will pay. After spending 20 years in a nuthouse, Luther leaves with a custom-filed and fitted set of metal chompers and a very negative view of humanity in general. In an agitated, gotta-bite-n-brood mood, Luther clucks like a chicken with a white-hot poker up its ass. He bites—they bleed—until the climactic cluck-off with a plucky farm wife who convincingly proves she's no ordinary chickenshit.

Many smaller films, for reasons known and unknown, simply slip beneath the radar and disappear into semi-obscurity, rescued only occasionally by rants delivered by devoted, and at times, seriously misguided film fanatics. Hmmm...know anyone like that? Most of these marginal flicks deserve their pariah status; but some are just too plain weird, unclassifiable or simply too fucked-up to escape at least some matter of notice by the genre press. These films, it seems, are often written about and summarily analyzed; sometimes for no better reason than to offer a plaintive warning to other fans. It's painfully obvious that numerous films are written up in the genre press simply to prove that they do, indeed, exist. Maybe the writer just wants to know if anyone else on the planet has also borne witness to such an embarrassing cinematic slag heap that simply defies criticism of any shade. All of these cast-off mutts do share at least one common bond: they have some indefinable *something* that causes them to get tangled up in one's memory — for better or worse.

One leading contender in the Cool Title/ Bitchin' Poster/Shitty Movie Sweepstakes would have to be *The Hollywood Meatcleaver Massacre (1976)*. This rare turd even managed to snag some old footage of venerable horror icon Christopher Lee introducing a tale decidedly not the one that is to follow. Lee has steadfastly denied any involvement with this film; though, of course, his name is featured prominently on the poster. The film aims high: it wants to be an *Exorcist/ Death Wish / Revenge-From-Beyond-The-Grave* amalgam; but it ultimately succeeds only in being a terrible, unconscionable waste of a kickass title. The film is so dark and grainy at times neither the meatcleaver nor the massacre have any impact whatsoever. There is an attack by a possessed cactus and one character does get a car hood slammed down repeatedly on him while he's changing the oil.

Despite being named Best Film of 1982 by the Academy of Science Fiction, Fantasy and Horror, *Night Warning* (aka *Butcher, Baker, Nightmare Maker*) never found its audience, perhaps lost in the torrential glut of slasher films released in the wake of *Halloween (1978)* and *Friday the 13th (1980)*. 'Tis a pity too, because despite its *de riguer* big knife mayhem, the film boasts an incendiary performance by Susan Tyrell; one of the most harrowing car crashes ever staged; and enough sly twists and turns to keep it reasonably suspenseful to the very end. Bo Svensen is risibly effective as the homophobic sheriff out to prove Tyrell's girlyman nephew (Jimmy McNichol — yep, that one) is really a gay killer. Though the film's theme song, "Little Billy Boy" may cause you to perforate your eardrums with an ice pick, this is a slasher film in a class by itself. Director William Asher helmed nearly 100 episodes of *I Love Lucy* and was behind the camera on both *How to Stuff a Wild Bikini (1965)* and that towering trifle to teen twitdom, *Beach Blanket Bingo (1965)*.

David Winters' hip, witty and bloody *The Last Horror Film (1983)* benefits greatly by its shot-on-the-run footage of the 1981 Cannes Film Festival and by Joe Spinell's inspired turn as an obsessed New York cabbie (remember now, Spinell had a bit part in Martin Scorsese's *Taxi Driver*) hoping to convince Caroline Munro to star in his own self-produced movie, *The Loves of Dracula*. Winters' clever staging of numerous sequences blurs the line between what is real and what is "...only a movie..." and the dope smoking antics of Spinell's real-life mom, Mary, are a genuine hoot. There is also a slam-bang bit of smokin', spurtin' chainsaw mayhem that really delivers the grosseries. But was it... "only a movie?"

Perhaps the only human beings ever to witness the catastrophically inept, breathtaking bogosity, *Human Animals (1983)*, were in the audience that

Sunday morning when an obviously-pained promoter screened it for the members of L.A.-based Academy of Science Fiction, Fantasy and Horror. A scratchy, black and white, stock footage montage of nuclear explosions offers a feeble excuse for a global holocaust that leaves four survivors stranded on a remote island. The hopes of all humanity rest on these chosen few: one babe, two guys and a German Shepherd. The film chases its tail around until the girl sets up housekeeping with the dog and the two dudes are left taking turns dropping the soap in the shower. After the screening, the film's distributor apologized profusely to the stunned audience, still glued to their seats in slack-jawed disbelief.

Some films have so many strikes against them, it's a minor miracle they're ever screened, let alone remembered. *Bloodsucking Freaks in Pittsburgh (1990)* is guilty on numerous counts: (1) It sat on the shelf for years; (2) The director removed his name from the film; and (3) It's a goddamn "horror-comedy." It started as *Picking Up the Pieces* and was supposed to be a contemporary reworking of H. G. Lewis' infamous *Blood Feast (1963)*. The film chronicles the antics of a fez-topped Egyptian psycho killer who's collecting body parts for use in an arcane ritual (oh, surprise, already!). A couple of braindead detectives join a cop's daughter in the search for the maniac, as the film pushes its "R"-rating to the max with a grisly, gore-soaked tableaux of interpersonal carnage orchestrated by Pittsburgh's own Tom Savini. Besides the usual decapitations, dismemberments and face-peelings, the film offers a hilariously sadistic Stop Smoking clinic; death by industrial vacuum; autopsy parties; and a boner-

inducing, leather-clad chainsaw slut (ex-porn star Veronica Hart) reduced to pervo-puree in a giant hydraulic press. The real "Alan Smithee" would be pleased.

Resourceful horror fans often turned toward foreign shores when Stateside products turned sour and predictable. Although few of these films would ever be shown here theatrically, most would be tough to find even on domestic video or DVD. Fortunately, especially for Lifelong Seekers of the Bloody Grail, many of these titles would be made available by small, enterprising mail-order companies that specialized in the really weird, criminally insane shit that some collectors crave. The Red Sea was parted, and the Crimson Tide splashed ashore on every known continent. And all too often, when budgets precluded the use of even entry-level special effects work, some foreign actors came face to face with real beasts, bugs and bloodshed.

Look out for *Centipede Horror (1989)* if you've never experienced an Asian fast food feast that includes centipede (the really big kind) scarfing, scorpion barfing and all manner of slimy, crawling, wriggling insect life emerging from orifices they simply have no business being in. These bug-assed, creepy-crawly crowd scenes employ no mechanical impostors; they're real as hell, and in this twisted spectacle, they're usually partying right there in your mouth. The addition of several sequences showcasing an airborne, dive-bombing squadron of burning, re-animated chicken skeletons that perform precision maneuvers on command only sweetens this strange brew.

From Indonesia, Jalil Jackson's *Lady Terminator (1988)* comes out firing on all cylinders.

SMOKIN' IN THE GIRLS' ROOM...*Rabid Grannies.*

Merging a modern, John Woo-styled shooting safari with an ancient, mythic, black magic "Legend of the South Seas Queen," this wack-o flick simply pummels the viewer with an eclectic barrage of imagery as weird as it is oddly compelling. The film's all over the place, beginning "Somewhere in the South Seas" and climaxing cityside with several thunderous shootouts instigated by a hot babe in a skin-tight, studded leather, *Mad Max*ine-styled bondage outfit brandishing a smokin' M-16. Because this Terminator is also a lethal temptress, a bunch of horn dog boneheads end up both dickless and abandoned. There are tons of cool crashes, big explosions, weird sex, a hefty body count and a knockout climax sure to become legend. During a particularly furious firefight, this bodacious babe pokes her own eyeball out, gets blown up by a huge gas explosion and comes back for more as a toasted, crispy critter with glowing orbs that shoot killer laser beams. *Whew*.

Fans of the muscular, kung fu star of the legendary *Story of Ricky (1991)* will surely not want to miss Stanley Tong's Hong Kong delight, *Stone Age Warriors (1990)*. Set in the jungles of New Guinea, this bracing stew mixes martial arts; mercenaries; cannibals; slick chicks; giant scary lizards; huge fat-assed toads; and plenty of unscripted barfing; in addition to the casual, charismatic charm of Fan Siu Wang, the ol' Rickeroo hisself. Most versions circulated in the U.S. featured hilarious outtakes under the credits showing two scared-shitless ingenues blowing lunch for real when a stunt monitor lizard (think Kimodo dragon) gets loose and heads for their skirts.

Brazilian filmmaker Fauzi Mansur brought back the good ol' fashioned gore film with a vengeance by the near simultaneous Stateside release of both *Satanic Attraction (1990)* and *The Ritual of Death (1990)*. Though the latter film packs more of a wallop, be sure to catch the eye-popping trailer (included on the factory pre-records) for *Satanic Attraction* that plays like a Greatest Hits Package of Splatterdom's Wettest Moments. Both films feature generous gore; kinky sex (the tryst in a bloody-bathtub-with-severed-goat's head is a real keeper); flamboyant, Argento-inspired visuals; and double-digit body counts.

Though the much-reviled "horror-comedy" has suffered much critical abuse through the decades, the anthology film is usually greeted by pundits with equal disdain. Very few succeed, and those that do are usually wildly uneven. Higher profile, star-driven attempts like *Creepshow (1982)*, *The Twilight Zone: The Movie (1983)*, *Creepshow 2 (1987)* and *Two Evil Eyes (1990)* bear this out—the whole always seems far less than the sum of its parts.

The surprisingly accomplished *Night Train to Terror (1985)*, which credits five directors, scores mightily in each of its three segments, two of which were culled from full-length features. The third, "The Case of Harry Billings," was assembled from an unfinished feature starring John Philip Law, caught up in a black market organ transplantation ring. As both God and Satan debate metaphysical issues aboard a train packed with teenage rock & rollers in the film's linking device, a catchy, frothy pop confection, "Everybody's Got Something to Do," introduces each of the three segments. The episode cut down from the feature-length *Death Wish Club (1983)*, showcases a group of suicide-savvy hipsters out to off themselves in the most colorful and creative fashion possible. A Nazi war criminal may indeed be the Antichrist in the segment drawn from the ambitious, but belabored *Cataclysm: The Nightmare Never Ends (1980)*, which again proves that often, less is more. *Night Train* offers plenty of

gleefully gory FX; grisly dismemberments; organ snarfing; on-the-spot amateur heart surgeries; and a bit of really crappy stop-motion animation that only adds to the wacky, surreal, good time fun. During the simply underwhelming climax, a toy model train crashes off a table—only to quickly reappear—chugging skyward, apparently on its way to a celestial reward, as the closing theme drones on. Don't hold the limp dick ending against this modest treat just because, "Everybody's got something to do...everybody but *you!*"

Jeff Burr's feature film debut, *The Offspring (1986)* (aka *From a Whisper to a Scream*) is a kickass, taboo-trashing splatfest that throws up (literally) such a twisted slate of corpse fucking; Confederate cannibal kids; rotted zombie babies and razor-eating freakazoids that it's practically transcendent. The four segments are linked by an ineffectual side story wasting the talents of both Vincent Price and Susan Tyrell; but it's a small price to pay, and the distraction is only fleeting. For a change, all the episodes are well-written, capably acted (Clu Gulager and Cameron Mitchell, especially—never finer) and dripping with assorted precious bodily fluids. Burr went on to direct the confoundingly bizarre *Eddie Presley (1990)* as well as *Leatherface (1990)* and *Pumpkinhead 2: Blood Wings (1994)*.

Seek then, and ye shall find; untold, twisted treasures just waiting to be unearthed again and again by successive generations of gorehounds bound together on their Holy Sanguinary Journey.

BUDDY'S HERE

Slaughterhouse

© copyright 1987

AMERICAN ARTISTS INC.

MINDY CLARKE BECAME A POSTER GIRL FOR SEXY SADOMASOCHISTIC DEAD TEENS
WITH HER PIERCING PERFORMANCE IN BRIAN YUZNA'S *Return of the Living Dead 3*.

DAWN OF THE ZOMBIES

Imagine a world without the blank-eyed, rotting, shuffling snarfers of human flesh, these denizens of Zombie Nation, this Legion of the Dead. Go ahead, try it. You can't and it's George Romero's fault. If he hadn't made the greatest trilogy of *Dead* pictures of all time, the cinematic zombie just might have clumsily stumbled off into the sunset and joined the cowboy flick and the musical in the dustbins of movie lore. Romero single-handedly rocked the world of the living dead, establishing an unswerving template of ambulatory necrophagi that has been slavishly copied by legions of writers, directors, and make-up FX artists for well over 30 years.

Eschewing the voodoo origins of many of the early zombie films, Romero's zombies were re-animated by radiation from a foiled space probe, unleashing an army of the freshly dead as cannibalistic connoisseurs of non-selective carnage. These zombies had no game plan. They were simply hungry. If you were still alive, you entered the new food chain, at the bottom. Parent, child, lover, brother, hero became simple zombie fodder. Later, as Romero began extrapolating his theories on the living dead, zombies became metaphors, mirroring a decaying culture's mindless consumerism and savagely mocking society's herding instincts.

With *Day of the Dead (1985)*, Romero introduced yet another twist to the formula: a semi-educated, literary, music-loving zombie who tried to make the absolute most out of his condition. A real original prototype of the self-aware, proactive, multi-tasking deadhead. Perhaps even you, dear reader, know one of these guys. Before Romero raised the stakes on this long-established subgenre of the horror film, zombies had a decidedly lower profile. After *Night of the Living Dead (1968)*, the living, walking, chomping dead would never, ever be the same. Like I said, blame the Big

Guy from Pittsburgh.

Actually, the zombie film has been one of the most resilient staples of the horror film, introduced right alongside the iconic creatures found in *Frankenstein (1931)*, *King Kong (1932)* and *Dracula (1932)*. *White Zombie (1932)*, directed by Victor Helperin, starred Bela Lugosi as "Murder Legendre," a Haitian sugar plantation overlord whose workers put a new and different bite into the term "dead time."

Another towering icon of early screen scares, Boris Karloff, also made numerous films exploiting his haunted, otherworldly visage in a series of films addressing the nascent undead life-after-death issue. Karloff wasn't really a zombie in *Frankenstein*, though he was one dead dude; but in the British film *The Ghoul (1933)*, Karloff is a re-animated Egyptologist, back-from-the-dead to avenge the theft of a sacred jewel. Karloff continued to mine the crypts of the living dead in such films as *The Walking Dead (1936)*, *The Man They Could Not Hang (1939)* and *The Devil Commands (1941)*.

Other well-known thespians frequently entered the Arena of the Dead, and even the legendary Erich von Stroheim played a lovesick, vengeful surgeon who dabbles in the black arts in *The Crime of Dr. Crespi (1935)*. Dwight Frye, echoing his role as Fritz in the original *Frankenstein*, plays a graverobber assisting the Doctor's attempts at re-animation.

The Halperin brothers, the creative team behind *White Zombie* (and caught up in the newly fanned flames of a developing subgenre) delivered *Revolt of the Zombies (1936)*, introducing a secret army of living dead soldiers employed by the French in World War II on the Austrian front. The film was delivered DOA to the nation's box offices and it wasn't long before the living dead were really dying in theatres across the country.

Jean Varbrough's splendidly titled *King of the Zombies (1941)* resurrected the idea of a zombie army created by a mad scientist on a remote island, but underwhelmed audiences beat the dead back into their graves.

A small measure of respect for the undead was regained by Jacques (*Cat People*) Tourneuri's sublime *I Walked with a Zombie (1943)*, which was genuinely creepy and potently atmospheric.

But it wasn't long before the freshly re-animated became fodder for foolishness, witness *Zombies on Broadway (1945)*.

Philip Ford's listless *Valley of the Zombies (1946)* did little to improve the lot of the ambulatory dead and soon genre filmmakers turned in masse to more fertile fields.

After World War II ended with a really, really big bang, movies eagerly embraced the newly-minted, Radioactive Animal/Insect Mutation Syndrome and the quiet, slow moving, low-profile zombie seemed destined to be buried yet again. For several decades, the living dead were not especially hostile, aggressive, really scary looking or even carnivorous. But, in an exhausted, paranoid Post War world, many, many things were to change...forever.

Though preceded by the abysmal *Zombies of Mora Tau (1957)*, Michael (*Conquerer Worm*) Reeves' *Castle of the Living Dead (1964)* and Sydney Salkow's *The Last Man on Earth (1964)*, an argument has been made to establish John Gilling's Hammer-produced *The Plague of the Zombies*

"BAR-BA-RA...THEY'RE COMING TO GET US ALL!"

(1966) as the first truly modern zombie film. The film is a richly atmospheric, moody potboiler that transcends its simple formula by introducing elements that would resonate in subsequent dead films for decades to come. The cinematography by Arthur Grant is rich with color and atmosphere, frequently jolting the viewer with jump cuts, jarring zooms with crash closeups, radical camera angles and dreamlike sequences drenched

The working class here is frequently the victim of aristocratic decadence and arrogantly exploited both in life and after death. The film also rattled some cages in the press corps and received several positive, if not necessarily breathless, reviews. "The best Hammer horror for some time," wrote the *Monthly Film Bulletin*. "The spell cast by *The Plague of the Zombies* is quite a potent one," said *Films and Filming*.

CANNIBAL BARBEQUE TIME LIGHTS UP THE *Night of the Living Dead.*

in heavily-filtered light. The edgy, revolutionary zombie makeup applied by Roy Ashton was famously highlighted during the signature graveyard resurrection sequence—a potent, spellbinding mo-ment endlessly recycled by lesser talents for decades to follow. The film also takes a political stance (later to be developed in Romero's trilogy) and mercilessly exposes the roiling emotions beneath the surface of internecine class warfare.

But the review concluded with a telling caveat: "...but zombies have more or less been sucked dry as film material." Hmmm. We shall see.

Plague of the Zombies began by banging loudly on the doors. Two years later, Romero's film would splinter them.

Though the zombie film had been a staple of the horror genre for over three decades, little of what came before could possibly prepare audiences for Romero's bleak, ultraviolent, nihilistic tale of a world run amok. No longer were zombies singularly conjured by arcane rituals; but now, instead, in Romero's Brave New Dead World, they were re-animated *en masse* by a mysterious radioactive space probe and, man, were they hungry!

Night of the Living Dead (1968) broke down any and all remaining barriers of the zombie film and rewrote a brand new script for the Ages. His film provided a visionary glimpse of a societal apocalypse as a Hell on Earth that shockingly transcended the frequently feeble worm-churners that meekly preceded it. When one of the lead actors becomes zombiefied quickly in the first act and attacks his sister during a graveyard disturbance, you just know All Bets Are Off.

Romero was just simply rewriting all the rules. His zombies were no longer the shuffling legions of faceless, anonymous automatons; but rather friends, family and loved ones who had crossed The Line and had now returned to seek you out, bite your face off and gobble up your soft parts. In establishing this new Beachhead for the Dead, Romero's zombies were relentless, highly-motivated troops-from-the-tomb, threatening to overrun all strategic positions and bring the War of the Worms off the street and right into your living room. These dead fucks were not just hungry... they were ravenous. They'd eat you, raw and runny if necessary, and fight over your steaming guts without thought and without provocation. The simple *reductio ad absurdum* was finally applied to this new Darwinian Doctrine of the Dead...We Will Eat You!

The simple fact that the film's nominal hero was black was often cited in an attempt to bolster the film's underlying themes of class alienation, social consciousness and political upheaval, but Romero has always maintained Duane Jones was hired simply because he was the best actor to audition for the part. When Jones survives the *Night of the Living Dead* only to be shot dead at dawn's early light by a posse of redneck avengers, Romero really pulls the rug out from beneath his audience.

Night of the Living Dead was, most assuredly, a product of the times, tapping into the zombie zeitgeist of one of the more troubled, divisive decades in our history. Rocked by the Cuban Missile Crisis, reeling from a presidential assassination, torn asunder by civil rights demonstrations and riots, becoming more deeply involved in a winless war in Indochina, and witnessing the dissolution of the American nuclear family, the nation was, indeed, at war with itself.

The disturbing scenes of graphic gore and cannibalism, as well as its robust body count and depressingly amoral viewpoint, forced many viewers to confront demons they didn't even know existed. Romero didn't care. He was busy rewriting the Book of the Dead for generations as yet unborn. Made for just less than $100,000, *Night of the Living Dead* was the watershed zombie film of its time and Romero's bloody paw prints were to be splashed over nearly every dead film from then on. Zombies were back from the grave...and ready to party!

Because Romero had been so successful in deconstructing the traditional zombie film, future filmmakers were freed to experiment with various scenarios involving zombies from nearly all walks of life...and death. The Rotted Ones could now be

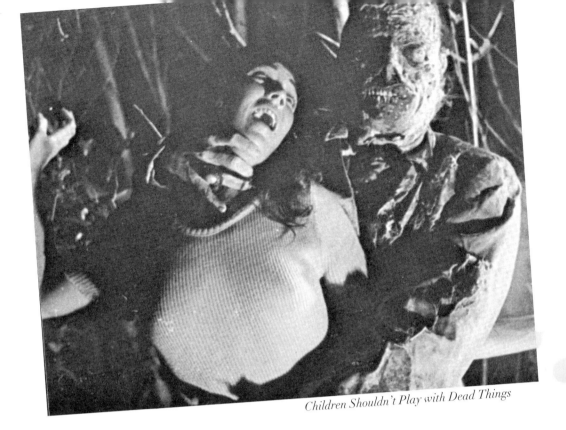

Children Shouldn't Play with Dead Things

young, old, or in-between. They could be soldiers, bikers, priests, virgins, rednecks, rock & rollers or vivisectionists. They could walk and run, use tools, fly airplanes, ride horses, read books, go to high school, play kick-ass heavy metal dirges, be a cop or bone your girlfriend.

The re-animation process was similarly liberated from its Third World voodoo origins and now zombies could be conjured by a plethora of both old and new world devices.

Filmmakers ran with it and the freshly dead were revived by cryptic incantations, blood sacrifice, drugs, radiation, toxic waste, ten-inch-railroad-spikes-in-the-brain, nerve gas, infrasound waves and rock & roll music. Some came back to life without an explanation — or apology — and gnoshed with the best of 'em from the Old School. Even the two most revered dictums from Romero's film: "They're dead. They're all messed up." and "Shoot 'em in the head!" were no longer

universally applicable. Some weren't messed up at all. They were crafty, fearless, versatile, tool-using saboteurs, totally committed to chaos and chronic violations upon both people and property.

Soon, some of the more upwardly mobile deadheads could also talk, think, reason, shave, operate a police radio, discharge weapons, have pets and enjoy oral sex.

The old, reliable gunshot-to-the-head, the dictum that reasoned that "you kill the brain, you kill the ghoul," was also severely tested. These New Age Wormheads could now survive multiple gunshots, decapitations, bodily dismemberment, dissection, bisection, brain removal and assault by sharp-edged weapons. They developed a taste for not just human flesh, but for culture as well, voraciously feeding an aching appetite for music, brains, sex, revenge, and contemporary culture.

Night of the Living Dead proved itself "The Shot-in-the-Head Heard 'Round the World."

THEY JUST *won't* LISTEN BECAUSE *Children Shouldn't Play with Dead Things*.

And the '70s began in earnest with the emergence of a new, improved zombie fever slowly spreading its putrescent tendrils throughout the globe. As the new decade began, zombies were hot and they were all over the place—from graveyards to galleons, from battlefields to seashores—the dead came, they cannibalized and they conquered.

Stateside, Bob Clark (who would later direct the breakthrough teen gross-out comedy *Porky's*) helmed the raggedy, cartoonish *Children Shouldn't Play With Dead Things (1972)*, followed by the

haunting, troubling *Deathdream (1974)*. *Children*, though creepily effective at times, is nearly capsized by the buffoonish, nails-on-the-blackboard performance of Alan Ormsby (co-writer and now a top Hollywood scripter) as a theatre troupe's leader whose cryptic incantations raise an army, or at least a platoon, of the living dead. When Ormsby finally shuts his yap, his highly-effective zombie makeup and special effects work speak for themselves. *Deathdream* (aka *Dead of Night*, *The Night's Walk*), a contemporary reworking of the classic W.W. Jacob's short story, "The Monkey's Paw," introduces a Vietnam War-era zombie soldier finally returning home, to expectedly disastrous results. Viewed by many as an allegory of the disintegration of the traditional nuclear family unit in the traumatic wake of the Vietnam War, the film also introduced the grisly special makeup effects of a major player soon to become a household name in the House of Horror: Tom Savini.

Soon, Europe, especially Italy and Spain, was infected with the spreading zombie virus which seemed to permutate even further, as various cultures and societies put their own unique spin on Modern Maggot Mayhem. The Spanish/Italian coproductions *House of the Living Dead (1971)*, *Return of the Zombies (1971)* (costarring redoubtable Spanish horror icon, Paul Naschy) and Armando Crispino's *The Dead Are Alive (1972)* added a decidedly international flavor to the simmering stew. But it was Amando D'Ossorio's *Blind Dead* series that injected the burgeoning subgenre with a welcome dose of originality and swaggering bravado. Tombs of the *Blind Dead (1971)*, *Return of the Evil Dead (1973)*, *Horror of the Zombies (1974)* and *Night of the Seagulls (1975)* proved an indispensable link in the evolution of the Euro-zombie thriller.

Ossorio's hooded, eyeless, skeletal apparitions, found frequently on horseback, were based on a radical religious order formed in the early 12th century to protect pilgrims en route to the Holy Land during the First Crusade. The Knights Templar, these soldiers of Christ, soon became one of the most disciplined, most-feared fighting forces on the continent. For nearly two hundred years, these Monastic Marines, existing in nearly autonomous conditions, gradually became law unto themselves. Drunk with power, the Templars were nearly unstoppable until a series of brutal, corrupt campaigns brought them to their knees in French courts in 1307. A litany of charges including blasphemy, devil worship, abortion and sodomy were brought against the Templars and soon hundreds were being imprisoned, tortured, and burned alive. Five years after the Templar Roundup had commenced, both the Grand Master and his Vice Prez were ritually slow-roasted over a roaring fire.

Ossorio has always insisted that his resurrected Templars were not even real zombies, but "mummies on horseback." Many would, and still do, disagree. There is some credence, though, to a vampiric connection, as Ossorio's Templars would rise at night, seeking victims for the blood and not their flesh. Another unique Ossorio contribution to the Templar myth was that they were all sightless and had to locate their victims by sound alone. A spectral sonar, so to speak.

The *Blind Dead* films are also distinguished by their sublime sanquineousness and their bluntly overt juxtapositioning of sex, sadism, torture and blood quaffing. Many of Ossorio's Templars were partial to sacrificing teenage girls and ofttimes the combination of nudity and graphic violence proved overpowering to film watchdogs. Censored prints—leaving explicit scenes of dismemberment, beheadings, torture and heart removals on the cutting room floor—were widely circulated and, only recently, through the magic of DVD was the missing footage finally restored. Most aficionados find *Return of the Zombies* to be the most fully realized episode; but each and

BREASTS 'N' BLOOD—STAPLES OF EUROHORROR, IN JORGE GRAU'S SPLENDID
The Living Dead at Manchester Morgue / Let Sleeping Corpses Lie.

ANOTHER VICTIM OF THE MESSY EATING HABITS OF THE RECENTLY DECEASED
AND REANIMATED CORPSES OF *Living Dead of Manchester Morgue.*

every chapter contains generous helpings of stunningly beautiful set pieces, hallucinatory horror and arthouse splatter sure to move even the most demanding Euro-horror hound.

The Spanish/Italian co-production of Jorge Grau's *Living Dead at Manchester Morgue (1974)* (aka *Let Sleeping Corpses Lie*) proved to be yet another unique and original take on the mythos of the dead. Grau's zombies become re-animated as the result of a secret government pest control program involving an ultrasonic extermination device that certainly proves effective, though with disastrous side effects. Then, at times, Grau bends his own zombie re-animation theory by allowing some of the apparently more privileged pus-heads to bring other corpses back to life by rubbing blood on their eyelids.

The radical gore quotient also quickly distinguished Grau's film from the pack, and soon, most prints in European circulation bore the telltale marks of the censor's scissors. Some of the gore effects still remain shocking, most especially in an initial encounter between an absentmindedly, daydreaming nurse yakking on the phone and a prowling zombie that climaxes with her breast being ripped off and carried away! Later a graphic evisceration results in some major entrail yanking and scarfing, while the guttee's eyeballs end up being chewed by the ocular aficionados of the living dead. One of the zombies shuffles about with a ghastly, groin-to-throat autopsy wound; and the various axe-whackings, eye-gougings and multiple gunshot wounds pushed the Red Tide to new levels of sanguinary superiority. The gore effects were handled by Gianetto de Rossi, soon to spill even more sauce in a series of groundbreaking

Italian zombie flicks directed by Lucio Fulci.

Living Dead at Manchester Morgue was released briefly in Stateside double and triple bills as *Don't Open the Window*, employing the same tagline: "...To avoid fainting, keep repeating..it's only a movie..." used previously in the *Last House on the Left* advertising campaign. Grau's film remains a real rarity—a thinking man's zombie film that kicked open the Gates of Hell even further.

Jean Rollin's artsy gore-romp *Raisins de la Morte (1978)* (aka *Pesticide*) explored the relationship between French wine, putrefaction and eco-catastrophe with decidedly mixed results.

The quiet, moody, confusing and highly-stylized *Messiah of Evil (1972)* borrows heavily from the George Romero playbook, essentially recreating *Night of the Living Dead*, using a small coastal California town as its primary *mis-en-scene*. Romero was again recalled when the film was reissued later, pilfering the tagline from *Dawn of the Dead*: "When there's no more room in hell..." Soon, under Romero's auspices, a Litigator of the Living Dead convinced the filmmakers to find another line. The director, William Huyck, and producer, Gloria Katz, went on to co-write and work on George Lucas' *American Graffiti (1973)* before Wild Bill committed career suicide by directing *Howard the Duck (1986)*.

British zombies rise up and chew the scenery in Amicus' twin tributes to William Gaines' infamous EC comics, *Tales from the Crypt (1972)* and *Vault of Horror (1973)*, doing little to advance the future possibilities of the zombie mythos.

Nazi zombies soon made one of their first big screen appearances in Ken Weiderhorn's creepy and effective *Shock Waves (1977)*, and later, unwise-

ly renewed their Actor's Guild cards with woebegotten Third Reich wormchurners like *Zombie
Lake (1980)* and *Oasis of the Zombies (1981)*.

The biggest, baddest, bloodiest dead film of
the decade was now just around the corner. And,
when this new zombie dawn broke, things were
never, ever going to be the same again. This particular Decade of the Dead reached a brain-splat-
tering, gut-snarfing, gore-drenched climax with
what is arguably The King Kong of the Cannibal-
Zombie World: George Romero's *Dawn of the
Dead (1979)*.

Just as his previous epic *Night of the Living
Dead* rewrote the textbooks on zombie lore, so too
would the epic towering *Dawn*, casting a shadow
so long and deep that nearly everything before it
was rendered in permanent eclipse. This swaggering and awesome chronicle of mass slaughter was
alternately brilliant, horrifying, fiendishly clever,
gut-wrenching, funny, meandering, self-reflective
and frivolous—sometimes all at the same time.
The wicked sense of fun, its subversive point-of-
view and its cartoonish excesses prevented *Dawn*
from just being a numbing, nihilistic bloodbath
and firmly positioned it as one of the most influential horror films of all times.

This is also the movie that made effects wizard
Tom Savini a household name (well, sort of....)
and effectively convinced an entire legion of
international filmmakers that they too could
apply Romero's winning formula to their dead
droppings.

The impact of *Dawn of the Dead* cannot be
overstated and the influence of its muscular
brand of mayhem has resonated globally now for
nearly 25 years. Along with only a handful of

other genre titles, most released within a few
years of one another, one can only marvel at just
how truly influential and catalytic these few
archetypical films would be. To attempt to chart
the subsequent permutations, copycats and rip-
offs of these few films that all clustered themselves at a similar point in time would be a staggering, butt-numbing endeavor. Imagine a world
without *Halloween (1978)*, *Alien (1979)*, *Dawn of the
Dead (1979)* and *Friday the 13th (1980)*. Within just a
couple of years, these four films changed the face
of modern horror forever.

Dawn proved to be an unqualified international hit (despite its self-imposed "unrated" status)
and European filmmakers, especially the Italians,
were taking copious notes. Lucio Fulci, a veteran
Italian director since 1959, had previously dabbled in a plethora of genres: comedies, westerns,
political potboilers, gangster flicks, supernatural
horror, outdoor adventures, and sex farces, and he
had proven that he could work fast. Since *Dawn
of the Dead* was released in the UK and much of
Europe as *Zombie*, *Zombies* or *Zombi*, Fulci
answered with *Zombies 2 (1979)* (aka *Zombie*,
Zombie Flesh Eaters, *Island of the Living Dead*) and
the Italian Cannibal Zombie tradition received its
bloody baptismal rites.

Zombie was shot quickly, for well under
$500,000 and rushed into theatres where it
became an international sensation. The American
one-sheet theatrical poster, featuring the lead
snaggle-toothed zombie festooned with an eye
socket full of worms bluntly confronted audiences
by screaming, "We are going to eat you!" Released
unrated, a stark disclaimer stated, "There is no
explicit sex in this picture. However, there are

scenes of violence which may be considered shocking." No fuckin' shit.

The simply outrageous set piece involving actress Olga Karlatos, a 14" splinter and one frisky attack zombie was a highwater mark in on-screen ocular apocalypse and remains one of the major gross-out shots of the decade. Fulci knew every-

Though *Zombie* made tens of millions of dollars in theatrical release, neither Fulci nor his FX artist, Gianetto de Rossi, made much dough. But, their go-for-broke attitude was ravenously received by gorehounds the world over and warmly embraced by the genre press. De Rossi has said that the minimal budget prevented him from

Tales from the Crypt WAS THE BEST AND MOST POPULAR OF THE AMICUS ANTHOLOGIES.

one would be waiting for the inevitable cutaway shot as he flashed alternate angles on both the wide-open, terrified eyeball and the approaching splinter, but the Maestro had something else in mind. Unflinchingly horrifying in intent and detail, the splinter not only slowly and deeply pierces the orb, but it breaks off in her eyeball, sending Karlatos shrieking into oblivion. There was no mistaking the dummy head when it was finally inserted in the sequence, but the absolute audacity and swaggering fearlessness of Fulci's approach was electrifying.

designing and applying latex prosthetics on the zombie extras so he went *au naturel*: "We used clay and pottery for the faces. The extras would come over in the morning and we'd cover them with the special mixture. Both Lucio and me used to refer to them as walking flower pots," explained de Rossi.

Other startling sequences, including a haunting graveyard resurrection; a very messy flesh feast; a simply surreal zombie vs. shark encounter; and numerous, splat-happy, oozing gaping wounds and cranial excavations betray the tiny

FX budget.

Though often thought of as a simple knee-jerk rip-off of Romero's *Dawn of the Dead*, Fulci's *Zombie* follows its own agenda. "I feel that *Zombie* is an authentic zombie film!" Fulci has said. "I wanted to send them back to their origins; this is why we shot the film in Santo Domingo. My inspiration came from Jacques Tourneur, not from Romero."

Fulci always felt Romero's zombies were used as metaphors for the alienated elements of civilization that existed on the fringes of society. "It's the revenge of the defeated from life," Fulci has said. "I truly think *Dawn of the Dead* is a political movie, a great movie, but different from my *Zombie*."

Fulci would follow with a triumvirate of zombie-themed supernatural thrillers that would cement his reputation as "The Maestro of Maggot Mayhem." Shot quickly on location in Savannah, Georgia, New Orleans and New England (interiors added later at De Paolis Studios in Rome), *City of the Living Dead (1980)* (aka *Paura della citta dei morti viventi*, *The Gates of Hell*); *The Beyond (1981)* (aka *L'Aldila*, *Seven Doors of Death*); and *The House by the Cemetery* (aka *Quella villa accanto al cimitero*) *(1981)*, were sublime, atmospheric zombie chunkblowers that also showcased Fulci's lifelong love of the work and themes employed by Edgar Allan Poe. *City of the Living Dead* also answers *Zombie*'s infamous eyeball scene with two major barf-baggers that involved the frequently cinematically-abused duo of John Morghen (Giovanni Lombardo Radice) and Daniela Doria. The former gets his brains drilled out his ears by an

IT'S ALWAYS DARKEST (AND BLOODIEST) BEFORE THE *Dawn*.

industrial drill press and the latter barfs up her entire intestinal tract. Though a prosthetic head was employed during the climactic stage of the effect, the actress still had to regurgitate some very real sheep innards bought at a local meat market. "Next to her is Michele Soavi (director of *Stagefright*, *The Church*, and *Dellamorte, Dellamore*) feeling sick," Fulci explained.

The Beyond, is arguably, Fulci's unassailable zombie masterpiece; a surreal splatfest that mixes hardcore carnage with magic realism. Fulci has stated, "It's a plotless film. There's no logic to it...just a succession of images."

When a woman (Katrina MacColl) inherits a Louisiana hotel, she finds out much too late that not only has the place a checkered past, but... but...it's built over one of the seven portals to

hell! While treating one of the early victims of the cursed place, a doctor (the late, great David Warbeck) begins investigating some of the mysterious occurrences and finds, indeed, that Hell Has Come to This House. Criminally short on logic and apparently operating with just a skeletal script, the film simply erupts at midstream and belches forth a series of horrifying, hauntingly bizarre imagery that buries the plot in a surreal flurry of sanguineous celebration. Again employing FX Maestro Gianetto de Rossi, the horror *frissons* here are the stuff of legend: gory crucifixions, chunkblowing chain-whippings, eyeball impalements, flesh-eating tarantulas, throat-shredding demon dogs, sulphuric acid meltdowns, ravenous zombies and the justifiably famous daylight-through-a-little-girl's-head cra-

WELL, GODDAMN! THEY'RE NOT EATING *us!* (*Zombie*)

WHEN THE POSTER ART FOR LUCIO FULCI'S *Zombie* SCREAMED: "WE ARE GOING TO EAT YOU!"—THEY *really* MEANT IT.

nial detonation apocalypse. Ah, yes, the splatter that *matters*.

Propelled by Fabio Frizzi's soaring, elegant symphonic score and rendered beautifully by Sergio Salvati's moody, atmospheric cinematography, *The Beyond* became Fulci's finest blueprint for Horror in the Third Degree.

In *The House by the Cemetery*, Fulci eschews most of the supernatural trappings of his previous features and greatly reduces the ranks of the living dead. A lone, flesh-eating freakazoid named Dr. Jacob Freudstein has returned from the netherworld and continues his dirty little experiments and bizarre surgical practices in the basement of a house recently inhabited by a New York couple and their young son.

Though not as outlandishly gory as previous efforts, *The House by the Cemetery* makes generous use of cranial catastrophes, maggot storms, and oozing riverlets of blood, pus and other unmentionable soft, wet things.

Fulci left zombies behind for years and explored a mixed bag of erotic thrillers, supernatural potboilers, futuristic fantasies and misogynistic slashers, but returned with an ersatz sequel (of sorts) with *Zombi 3* in 1988. Fulci had originally wanted to shoot it in 3-D, but producers had other plans. The film was shot in the sweltering, flesh-rending heat of the Phillipines and departed from Fulci's original voodoo/black magic approach and opted for re-animation via the accidental release of a powerful, experimental biological weapon.

The jungle locations and Asian zombies are disconcerting and the film stumbles aimlessly on its way to a lackluster finale. The gore quotient is

far below standards as well, and Fulci regularly complained afterwards that he absolutely hated the script. Reports vary widely, but Fulci left the production after five weeks and screenwriter Claudio Fragrasso and legendary hack director Bruno (*Hell of the Living Dead*) Mattei were called in to deliver a finished theatrical print. It's certainly not nearly as knockdown dreadful as some would insist, but the Fulci magic is conspicuously absent and the film never gels.

Besides Fulci, numerous other Italian filmmakers jumped into the arena, thrusting their arms elbow deep (and beyond) into the guts-n'-glory of zombiedom. Most of these films, produced at an alarming, truly hair-raising regularity, blew dead dogs in hell. Some were just so b-a-d they were, uh...just really fucked-up. Umberto (*Cannibal Ferox*) Lenzi's *Nightmare City (1980)* (aka *City of the Walking Dead*) featured clunky, pasty-faced ghouls departing an airliner and attacking the ground crew with all manner of sharp, cutting-edge hand tools. It's a sleazy mix of sex, gore and gratuitous godawfulness that's easy to resist. Since there's virtually no plot, it's a random and maddening mix of zombie attacks, topless skanks, cranial detonations, flesh-gnoshing, nipple-whacking and eye poking....all to little effect. The makeup looks like shit and the movie just chases its tail around for 90 minutes. Shoulda just shot itself in the head after the first reel.

Bruno Mattei's insufferable *Hell of the Living Dead (1980)* features the most boneheaded use of absolutely inappropriate stock footage in history, padding its already bloated 103-minute running time to bursting. Admittedly, the gore quotient is high: brains are blown out regularly; disembowl-

...e TU VIVRAI NEL TERRORE!

L'ALDILÀ

KATHERINE MacCOLL · DAVID WARBECK
SARAH KELLER · ANTOINE SAINT JOHN
e con VERONICA LAZAR

Prodotto da FABRIZIO DE ANGELIS per la FULVIA FILM srl

Regia di **LUCIO FULCI**

Technicolor

LUCIO FULCI BROUGHT
NEW LIFE AND A NEW
SENSIBILITY TO HIS TALES
OF THE WALKING DEAD.

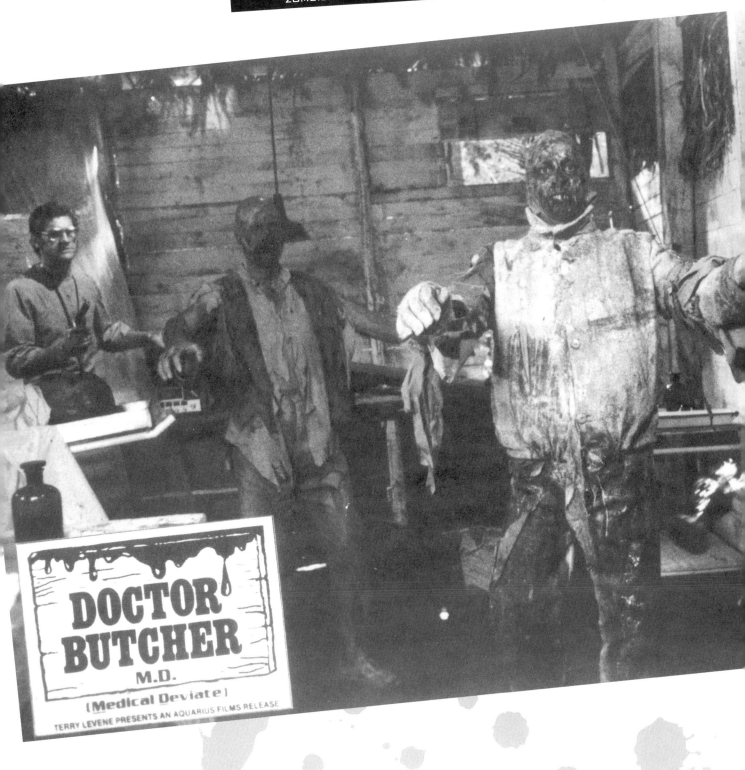

DOCTOR BUTCHER M.D.
(Medical Deviate)
TERRY LEVENE PRESENTS AN AQUARIUS FILMS RELEASE

ments and cannibalism run riot; and one character does get her eyeballs yanked out through her mouth, but its just a hurtfully bad piece of zombie detritus. At least Joltin' Joe D'Amato's *Erotic Nights of the Living Dead (1980)* has fucking (literally) zombies, masturbating females, frequent cannibal chowdowns and gore galore. So, if your tastes run to ribald, raunchy and utterly mindless amalgams of bad porno, cheapskate splatter and cheesy travelogue, this'll be a perfect fit.

Ofttimes in quicky exploitation fare, a filmmaker will strike a quirky combination of ineptitude, enthusiasm, luck and pluck and deliver a mutant progeny that you just have to take home with you. Fabrizio De Angelis, co-producer of Fulci's *Zombie*, began filming *Queen of the Cannibals* in late 1979, using the same locales—New York and Santo Domingo—as well as some of the leftover sets from Fulci's effort. Released to Italian theatres as *Zombie Holocaust (1980)*, this gleeful, balls-to-the-wall, gore-slinging delight has it all: dismemberments, heart removals, mad doctors, brain transplants, copious gut-gnoshing, eyeball poking, maggots, nudity and perhaps the finest facial puree by outboard motor ever committed to celluloid. And, as an added bonus, you get not just one but two of PastaLand's exploitation staples: zombies and cannibals! This frothing, heady stew was apparently not enough for American producer/distributor Terry Levene's Aquarius Releasing, though. He dumped the original soundtrack, spliced on a cheapjack prologue pulled from Roy (*Document of the Dead*) Frumkes' amateurish, unfinished anthology, *Tales That'll Tear Your Heart Out*, and retitled it *Dr. Butcher, M.D.*

The American poster featured an illustration of the legendary, Spanish surrealist painter Salvador Dali as the good Doc, replacing the master's paint brush with a bloody scalpel. A flatbed truck, dubbed "The Butchermobile," made the New York City rounds with dressed-up, suitably bloodied splat fans mugging beneath a banner that read, "I was operated on by Dr. Butcher!... and He makes House Calls!" Ah, True Art of the Highest Order.

Andrea Bianchi's *Nights of Terror (1980)* (aka *Zombie III, Burial Ground*) is a lovable mutt of a PastaLand chunkblower with gross-out FX; way-cool zombie makeup (by Gianetto de Rossi and Rosario Prestopino); living dead cannibal monks; and one butt-ugly, freakazoid dwarf zombie who bites mommy's nipple clean off!

When an archaeologist violates an ancient burial site, he's eaten alive by freshly-resurrected zombies, unleashing an army of the living dead into the countryside. These hyperactive, resourceful, tool-using zombies are real team players too—able to strategize and outwit their prey—before gang-gobbling numerous guests vacationing at an isolated country mansion. Crucifixions, dismemberments, disembowelments and major body carnage sets the screen awash in sauce; but one truly unforgettable scene illustrates the uneasy mix of sex, gore, cruelty, and fuckin' weirdness some of these PastaLand Putrefiers lovingly wallow in. The Bad Taste Bombshell (not necessarily a bad thing) here involved a really creepy 3o-something, four-and-a-half foot tall zombie stepson going dead-in-the-head on us and attacking mommy with a tit-shredding abandon that completely redefines the art of "breast feeding." The scene is

THE ZOMBIFICATION PROCESS APPARENTLY SPARED THIS SNAGGLE-TOOTH'S APPENDAGES.

achingly phony as all hell, but that's all part of *Nights of Terror's* simple, boneheaded charm.

An international flavor imbues Frank Agrama's *Dawn of the Mummy (1981)* and, though not strictly 100% Italian (U.S. and Egypt were marginally involved), it shows some real guts; a few hot babes; cool locations; and the very first cannibal / mummy / zombies (check me on this one) of the new Decade of the Dead. A new take on the res-urrection scenario as well—these zombies come back to life under the hot lights of a photo-shoot set up in a pharaoh's tomb by a bunch of snot-nosed fashion freaks. And, after a 3o-century snooze, these ravenous ragheads are simply not satisfied with skinny fashion models and immedi-ately head off to town for an all-you-can-eat desert buffet.

It takes awhile to get rolling, but once the munching mummies hit town, the guts hit the rotor blades with a studied fury. One poor guy is excitedly celebrating his wedding feast, but before he can consummate his marriage, the mummies take a bride and she's eaten before the hubby-ho-tep gets his shot. Rude, unconscionable behavior to be sure, but hey, dude, "They're dead...they're all messed up."

Not all Italian zombies are such misbehaving louts, though. Pupi Avati's *Zeder: Voices from the Beyond (1983)* (aka *Revenge of the Dead*) tries hard to be a sophisticated, supernatural thriller with zombies on the side. And if quasi-scientific rumi-nations on K-zones and immortality revealed through cryptic messages from an insane priest fries your burger, then you'll gladly listen to these voices too. All bark, though, with very little bite.

The Italian zombie film soon began running in circles until Lamberto Bava brought the dead back from a cinematic demise with *Demons (1985)*, a high octane, slambang gorefest, punctuated by a rowdy heavy metal score and a movie theatre packed to the rafters with the hungry undead. With some spectacular set pieces (cool helicopter crash through the auditorium's roof); grisly make-up and gore FX (by Sergio Stivaletti—the Italian Tom Savini); and the imprimatur of horror maestro Dario Argento, *Demons* rapidly restored faith to the faithless. While it's an academic conceit to debate the zombie vs. demon argument here, the

inevitable sequel, *Demons 2 (1987)* steered the series into the "demon puppet" arena, as hyperactive muppets on crack with anger management issues emerge from TV sets in a yuppie high rise and attack the self-absorbed, upscale lobsters. Fortunately, Bava powers the rampaging, putrescent puppets along at a feverish clip and one has little time to actually ponder just how stupid it all really is.

Andreas Marfori's wildly uneven *Evil Clutch (1988)* is yet another *Evil Dead* knockoff, but the combination of high-energy filmmaking; low-brow, cheesy (but splendidly saucy) FX; and a fearless disregard for logic and characterization prove largely irresistible. The splashy chainsaw eviscerations, multiple dismemberments, mashed

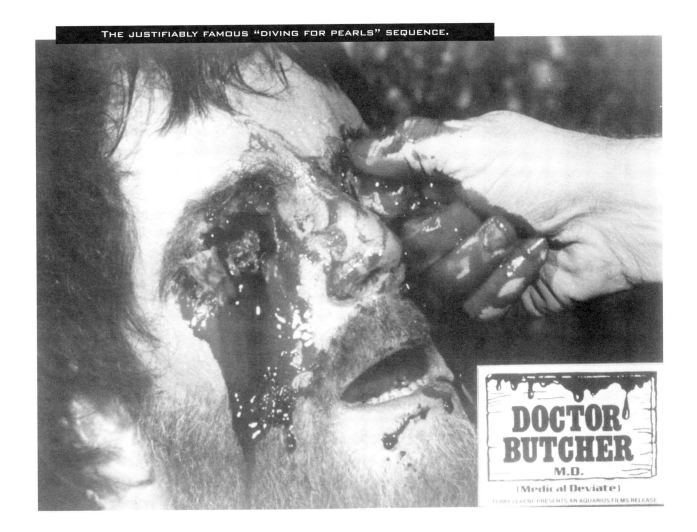

THE JUSTIFIABLY FAMOUS "DIVING FOR PEARLS" SEQUENCE.

DOCTOR BUTCHER M.D.
(Medical Deviate)
TERRY LEVENE PRESENTS AN AQUARIUS FILMS RELEASE

Lloyd Kaufman / Michael Herz
and the Troma Team present
an Agnese Fontana Production of an Andreas Marfori Film

EVIL CLUTCH

The Nightmare That Grabs You
Where You Least Expect It!

Una Produzione Fomar Film

R

© TROMA, INC. TROMA, INC.

noggins and chunkblowing elan, set amidst a sea of demon puke 'n' drool putrescence, should float any desperate gorehound's boat.

Claudio Fragrasso, the screenwriter on Fulci's troubled *Zombie 3*, helmed *After Death (1988)* (aka *Zombie 4*), and though the film is frequently mocked by Euro-Z connoisseurs, it remains a cheerful, eager-to-please, World-class chunkblower. With alarming regularity, eyes and heads are popped into pulp; heads and limbs are whacked off; and faces are peeled clean off as legions of clever, chunkbiting ninja-attack zombies prove Karnage is King. Exactly what one would expect from scientists trying to cure cancer on a remote island and conjuring zombies instead.

The crown jewel of the contemporary Italian zombie cinematheque is, undoubtedly, Michele Soavi's deliriously sublime *Dellamorte, Dellamore (1993)*, a stunning, but righteously moist, rumination on life, death, love, and love after death. Gorgeously photographed, with a riveting, compelling Rupert Everett as a conflicted cemetery watchman battling zombies ("Returners" here), Soavi's film (retitled *Cemetery Man* for U.S. release) is a heartbreaking, gut-churning, haunting work that many of the Euro Horror cognescenti deem the Greatest Italian Zombie Film of 'Em All. At the climax, however, the film takes a flying leap of faith and becomes either totally whacked or an unheralded surrealistic masterpiece.

Elsewhere in Europe and Asia, the dead also walked. *Devil Hunter (1980)* (aka *Manhunter*) starred a gigantic black zombie with ping-pong ball eyes who liked to nibble, chew, and eat pussy. No really...and he swallows! The living dead behind the camera included the Crash Zoom King of the

THIS PAGE: *Evil Clutch* LOW-BROW, CHEESY FUN.
FOLLOWING SPREAD: THE UNDERRATED *Dead and Buried* PROVES TO BE
A REAL KICK-IN-THE-RIBS FOR CURIOUS AFICIONADOS.

PROMOTIONAL POSTER ART FOR SAM RAIMI'S *The Evil Dead* FEATURED
SEVERAL SCENES THAT HAD NOTHING TO DO WITH THE MOVIE.

Known World, Jess Franco.

Jean Rollins' decidedly French take on the zombie mythos was *The Living Dead Girl (1982)*, a decidedly serious, artsy-fartsy meditation on lesbian zombie sisterhoods. It's impeccably filmed, well-acted, and is filled with atmospheric, dream-like *mis-en-scenes*, punctuated by scenes of ghastly gore. The film stars a sexy, self-reflective, conscientious corpse whose philosophical worldview is forever compromised when she eventually realizes her condition: "I am dead. I am DEAD!"

With major points given for originality and verve, Ho-Meng-Hua's *Revenge of the Zombies (1981)* (aka *Black Magic II*) is a thoroughly bent, audacious Asian entry featuring an evil sorcerer who subsists on human milk sprinkled with freshly shaved pubic hair. He controls a zombie legion by pounding ten-inch spikes into their brains and kicks them into hyperdrive by splitting his tongue with a huge knife and spitting blood at 'em. Yes, it is fuckin' weird...and then some.

Meanwhile, down in New Zealand, David Blyth's *Death Warmed Up (1984)* revisits the somewhat shopworn mad-doctor-on-a-remote-island scenario, but enlivens things considerably with an energetic, muscular style, cycle-riding zombies and lots o' fucked-up trans-cranial surgeries.

Fellow countryman Peter Jackson whose *Bad Taste (1989)* and *Meet the Feebles (1990)* had already set the world abuzz, dropped the Big One with *Braindead (1993)* (aka *Dead Alive*) — The Zombie Film of this or any other century. Here was the Ultimate Gore Film: the *Citizen Kane* of Karnage. The *Jurassic Park* of Putrescence. This swaggering, Herculean chunkblower is the stuff of legend. Here is, unequivocally, the *ce n'est plus ultra* of

modern splatter. Heads, limbs, and bodies are split and mashed with abandon; babies get pureed in blenders; ambulatory intestines take on a life of their own; and jealous zombie mommies have monstrous, flapping pussies that could accommodate a Ford Explorer. The righteous and justifiably famous "Toro Power Mower Living Room Zombie Massacre" splashes enough blood, guts and chunky soft parts to cover the state of Rhode Island to a depth of 11-inches. And, after this towering masterpiece of epic proportions, comes the *Lord of the Rings* trilogy. Now, Peter, what the fuck is up with that?

The double-dead zombie whammy generated by the near-simultaneous appearances of both *Dawn of the Dead* and *Zombie* did not go unnoticed by American filmmakers and the dead began rising on Yankee soil in fresh, new and exciting ways. For the next decade, the new American zombie would rock the planet.

Gary Sherman's moody, unsettling *Dead and Buried (1981)*, with a knockout script by Dan O'Bannon, returned the contemporary zombie into a *Twilight Zone*-styled realm of unlimited possibility. Though largely ignored during its initial theatrical run, the film looks better and better with age. A spunky, thoroughly engaging performance by Jack Albertson (in his final role) as the eccentric mortician of Potter's Bluff provides the film a solid ground on which to unleash a series of brutal, violent, undead-like behavior. Propelled by some really nasty FX by the then-unknown Stan Winston (the acid-up-the-nose gag and the hypo-to-the-eyeball especially); accomplished performances; a hypnotic score, and an absolute, fuckin' killer ending, *Dead and*

BRUCE CAMPBELL BECAME A GENRE ICON WITH HIS WITTY, HYPER-FRENZIED PERFORMANCE IN *The Evil Dead 2*.

Buried should be exhumed once again and sweetly savored. Watch closely and catch Robert Englund in one of his many pre-Freddy supporting roles.

Sam Raimi's frenetic, hot-wired *Evil Dead* (1982), smugly billed as the "ultimate experience in gruelling terror...," knocked both critics and fanboys' dicks into the dirt. Stephen King wet himself and heralded it as "the most ferociously original horror film" of its time. Though the storyline was feeble (suburban airheads find an arcane book in the woods and conjure demons), the storytelling was a headlong, jacked-up rush of pure adrenaline. Raimi's famous shakey-cam tracking shots (they tied their camera to a 2 x 4 and ran with it) and his complete and utter abandon with rules of zombie cinema helped make *Evil Dead*

appear far greater than the sum of its parts. The zombie re-animation and attack scenes were kick-ass examples of hi-octane, guerrilla filmmaking; and even the cheapjack, cheesy homemade special FX worked impeccably well. Raimi was clearly onto something here, but in future episodes his obsession with the Three Stooges, inane sight gags and boneheaded characters would steer the series into a zombie cartoonland.

Though *Evil Dead 2: Dead by Dawn* (1987) made the demon-beleaguered Bruce Campbell an international icon, the film played as though the original had never even happened—apparently to allow all the characters to make the same mistakes all over again. This gore-drenched, all-out FX spectacle tilts heavily towards humor rather than

THE WILD VARIETY OF MAKEUP FX SEEN IN *The Evil Dead 2* CALLED FOR THE SERVICES OF NEARLY A HALF DOZEN DIFFERENT SHOPS.

horror and this *Larry, Moe and Curly in the Haunted Forest* signaled an alarming trend in U.S. zombie lore.

Army of Darkness (1993) could have been titled *Medieval Dead* (Get it? Har...har) as Ash (Campbell) is dumped inexplicably back to the Middle Ages along with his trusty chainsaw, 12-gauge and '73 Olds. What the fuck here? Ash gamely battles armies of rubber skeletons on horseback, crappy blue-screen demons and Gumby-styled, stop-motion animated zombies. Some of the dialog is lame brained enough to make even the Stooges grind their teeth. This har-de-har-har horror hybrid was just too stupid for seasoned fans and just too goddamned weird for mainstream audiences, as evidenced by the two completely differ-

ent endings filmed for the movie. No need, though; they both blow. After a long series of mainstream mush and TV dalliances (he and partner Rob Tappert co-produced *Hercules* and *Xena: Warrior Princess*), Raimi found God and made *Spider-Man (2001)*. The sequel will make Raimi a gazillionaire. Good for him.

Long-in-the-tooth graybeard gorehound grandpas of the future will, no doubt, rock softly on their front porches and wax nostalgic, in animated terms, of a special time...and the memories of—That Zombie Summer. Released nearly simultaneously in a movie season like no other, Romero's epic *Day of the Dead (1985)*, Dan O'Bannon's electric *Return of the Living Dead (1985)* and Stuart Gordon's incandescent *Re-*

Animator (1985) almost stopped the earth from spinning on its axis. Again, what the fuck?

To accommodate budget restrictions involved in shooting a hyperviolent, gory, unrated film, Romero scaled down a proposed $10 million zombie apocalypse and set nearly all the action in an underground missile silo. Zombies outnumber humans 40,000-to-1 and small pockets of scientists, soldiers and civilians huddle beneath the surface and explore various schemes in dealing with the zombie plague. It's plenty talky, indeed, but the concepts presented are both compelling and persuasive.

Though more character-driven than the previous films, *Day of the Dead* still displays plenty of guts, as FX Maestro Tom Savini really comes of age with an amazing splatter platter of sliding guts, faceless zombie freaks, and provocative new makeups delivered with a chunkblowing gusto deserving of the highest praise. One of Romero's most original and daring creations, "Bub," an "educated" zombie who appreciates literature, Beethoven and human companionship, allows the film to explore hitherto uncharted waters.

Dan O'Bannon, whose previous script credits included both *Alien (1979)* and *Dead and Buried (1981)*, delivers a sexy, punk rockin', rocket-fueled zombie stomper with *Return of the Living Dead*, a (sort of) unofficial "sequel" to Romero's original. Top-notch performances (James Karen is a standout); cool makeup; hot, naked zombies; a smokin' soundtrack (spewing tunes from the Cramps, The Damned and 45 Grave); and a female half corpse who cries out for "More brains!," make This Return to the Land O' the Dead a most welcome journey.

Ken (*Shock Waves*, *Eyes of a Stranger*) Weiderhorn's brainless, groaningly unfunny, shit-headed mess of apocalyptic proportions, *Return of the Living Dead 2 (1988)*, nearly ended the series, but sequelmeister Brian Yuzna gamely resurrected it for the uneven, marginally memorable *Return of the Living Dead 3 (1993)*. Echoing Romero's military/scientific aspects of zombie control, Yuzna's undead are being experimented on as possible warriors in a secret laboratory complex near Los Angeles. The experiments go wrong, horribly wrong (who woulda thunk?) and our young, heroic couple (she's dead, he's not) is then relentlessly (or is it endlessly) pursued through the city's sewer system by soldiers, cops, gangbangers and zombies.

Yuzna's film made Mindy Clarke a mayo-spilling, fanboy poster girl for her portrayal of a conflicted, topless, fetishist zombie whose body has been ritually pierced, sliced, and scarred by nails, scrap metal, broken glass and razor wire.

Stuart Gordon's career with the experimental Organic Theatre in Chicago took a jolting hit when he and producer Brian Yuzna began filming *Re-Animator* based on a six-part series of pulp fiction by H. P. Lovecraft, loosely gathered under the title "Herbert West: Re-Animator."

Jeffrey Combs plays West as a full-tilt, megalomaniacal superstar scientist at Miskatonic Medical School who believes his glowing, chartreuse "reagent" can raise the dead. It can, indeed, but with dire results, 'natch. Since producer Yuzna has never been shy about his affinity for seeing decapitated heads being carried about, *Re-Animator* gave him a shot at showing both the revolting and erotic aspects of the recently head-

BEFORE AND AFTER SHOTS
OF A HOME SURGERY-STYLED
CRANIAL BISECTION.

Army of Darkness PROVED TO BE TOO WEIRD FOR MAINSTREAM AUDIENCES
AND NOT NEARLY SCARY ENOUGH FOR SPLATTER AFICIONADOS.

A DECIDEDLY MOTLEY CREW OF DEMOGRAPHICALLY INCORRECT ZOMBIES INVADE THE UNDERGROUND SILO DURING THE GUT-CRUNCHING FINALE OF *Day of the Dead*.

less. Besides presenting what was undoubtedly the first instance of a freshly-shorn "head giving head," both Gordon and Yuzna registered yet another screen first: the fatal strangulation of a main character by a thrashing, hyper re-animated 25-foot coil of exploded intestines.

Re-Animator is a pure, unfettered delight, one of the best, brightest, bravest and wettest Horror Films of the Modern Era.

Yuzna's *Bride of Re-Animator (1990)* never bothers to explain how Herbert survived a seemingly fatal attack by malevolent, hot-wired guts in the original, but gets both West and his erstwhile lab partner Dan Cain (Bruce Abbott), busy right away building the beast. No longer content with re-animating parts, Herbert is after the entire enchilada here; he wants to create an entirely new life in the laboratory. Kathleen Kinmont's heart-rending, terminally-tragic turn as the Bride keeps the film on track as the tone is continually battered between the quasi-surreal, goofball creations of Screaming Mad George and the sublime, delicately detailed Bride by KNB EFX.

Many zombie films contain healthy dollops of both horror and black humor, usually with decidedly mixed results, but Fred Dekker's debut feature, *Night of the Creeps (1986)*, manages to successfully juggle both, with a savvy, understated aplomb. With characters named after famous horror directors and featuring a compelling combination of exploding heads, alien sluggettes and axe-wielding zombie fratboys, this amalgam of *Rock-'n'-Roll High School* and *Night of the Living Dead* is a modest, deliciously moist delight.

Depending on one's definition of what constitutes a "living dead" state of mind, a case could be

made for *Maniac Cop (1987)* and its two sequels: *Maniac Cop 2 (1990)* and *Maniac Cop 3: Badge of Silence (1992)*. Alive, dead or undead, series star Robert Z'Dar as the avenging Porker from Hell, is one freaky-lookin' mo'fo' with or *without* makeup.

For years, the voodoo mystique of zombie lore was largely ignored in favor of flashier, more modern techniques of re-animation. Wes Craven's *Serpent and the Rainbow (1988)* revisits those roots in an effective, and, at times, chilling film based on anthropologist Wade Davis' 1985 book about a search for a mysterious Haitian "zombi" potion. Davis sought to place zombification within a cultural context (termed "vodoun" here) and perhaps uncover a natural surgical anesthetic that could be refined for medical usage.

Craven follows along those lines for awhile, but cannot resist his now-familiar "dream sequence" inserts and also seems intent on delivering *Raiders of the Lost Ark*-style pyrotechnics at the climax despite the film's decidedly unspectacular premise. The teeth-rattling sequence in which Bill Pullman is buried alive and entombed with a huge tarantula remains a real corker.

Mary Lambert effectively renders Stephen King's *Pet Sematary (1989)* as a contemplative, noirish thriller, despite having to juggle zombie cats, homicidal dead kids and characters who simply refuse to learn from their deadly fuck-ups. Lambert returns to the moldy grounds of the creepy ol' Indian burial grounds and introduces a new cast of dimwits in *Pet Sematary 2 (1993)* and makes absolutely no apologies for the cast's ignorance of the original King book, the first movie, nor the theme of "A Monkey's Paw." These clueless shitheads wouldn't recognize a real zombie if

THE TALKING TRASH HALF-CORPSE KNOWS WHAT IT TAKES TO START THE PARTY: "MORE BRAINS!"

LEFT: LINNEA QUIGLEY FANTASIZES WHAT IT'S LIKE "TO DIE HORRIBLY, VIOLENTLY" IN DAN O' BANNON'S ROCK SOLID *Return of the Living Dead.*

PREVIOUS PAGE: KEN WIEDERHORN'S MUCH-REVILED, CLUELESS *Return of the Living Dead II* NEARLY SHUT THE LID ON THE COFFIN OF THE AMBULATORY CORPSE FLICK.

Return of the Living Dead II

one yanked their intestinal tract out of their smug, little, self-absorbed asses. They just still don't get it.

At least Bill Hinzman's oddly watchable *Revenge of the Living Zombies (1989)* gets it—if you're going to steal material, pilfer the best stuff available. Hinzman was the blank-faced, shuffling graveyard zombie in Romero's original *Night of the Living Dead* and he's back here as a real multi-tasker: producer, director, editor, star and zombie gut-gobbler. Nothing new here; it's good, stupid fun, though, and gory as hell. The film's guileless

sense of wonder and refreshing unpretentiousness prove welcome relief in light of the misfired color remake of Romero's venerable *Night of the Living Dead*.

Armed with a half-assed, perfunctory script by Romero himself; with a superstar FX demigod at the helm; and hotshit, new computer-manipulated zombie designs on board, the 1990 version of *Night of the Living Dead* thudded into theatres and just laid there—Dead on Arrival. Director Tom Savini, Romero and the producers all have had their say, but no matter who's at fault, perhaps the

174

Return of the Living Dead II

most telling reason was Romero's admission that "my interest...was purely financial."

Romero and Savini again teamed up for a tepid, lackluster retelling of Edgar Allan Poe's "The Facts in the Case of M. Valdemar" in *Two Evil Eyes (1990)*, coupled with Dario Argento's take on "The Black Cat." Romero's tale is an anemic rehash of the musty revenge-from-beyond-the-grave scenario that had already been beaten to death in an overexposed run of stories in EC Comic's "The Vault of Horror" and "Tales from the Crypt," as well as bludgeoned again recently in Romero's own *Creepshow (1982)*. Once again, the walking dead were looking in need of a long, long rest.

The Dead Pit (1991) was a frisky, nuthouse zombie potboiler with legions of lobotomized experiments rising from the Basement of Failed Surgeries to snack on shrieking, and sometimes scantily-clad, hospital personnel. However, the film will probably best be remembered for its gaudy 3-D video box, featuring a generic zombie with blinking red eyes.

The Dead Hate the Living! (2000) was a promis-

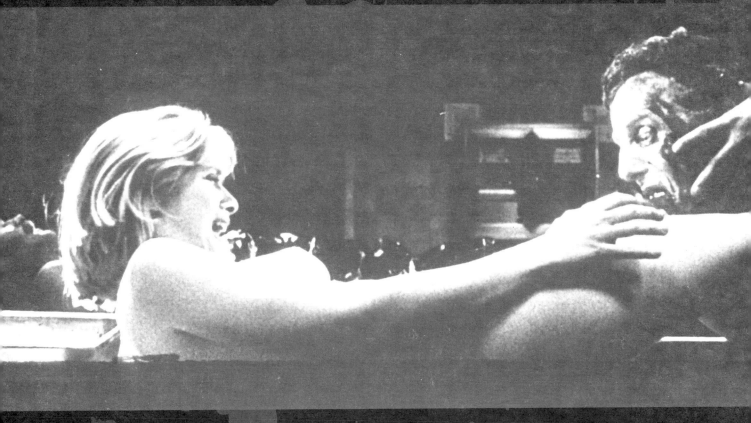

THE INFAMOUS "HEAD GIVING HEAD" SEQUENCE FROM STUART GORDON'S *Re-Animator.*

"DEATH IS ONLY THE BEGINNING," CLAIMS
NEW SURGEON-ON-THE-BLOCK, DR. HERBERT WEST.

CAN A TALKATIVE, SEVERED HEAD REALLY
SATISFY THIS NUBILE INGENUE?

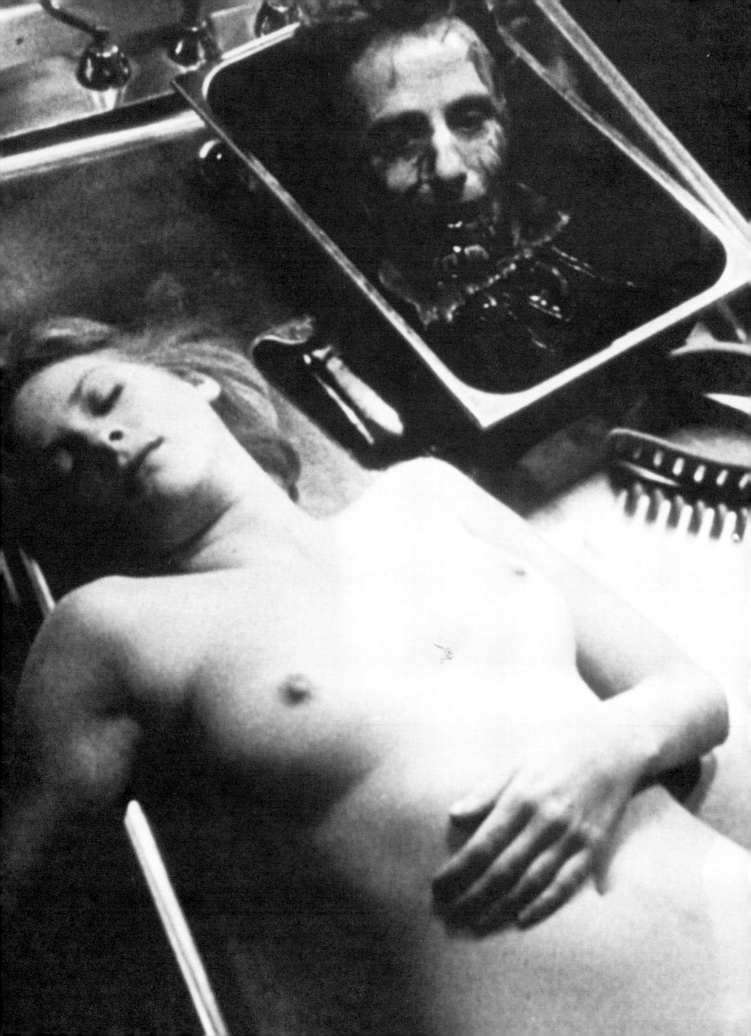

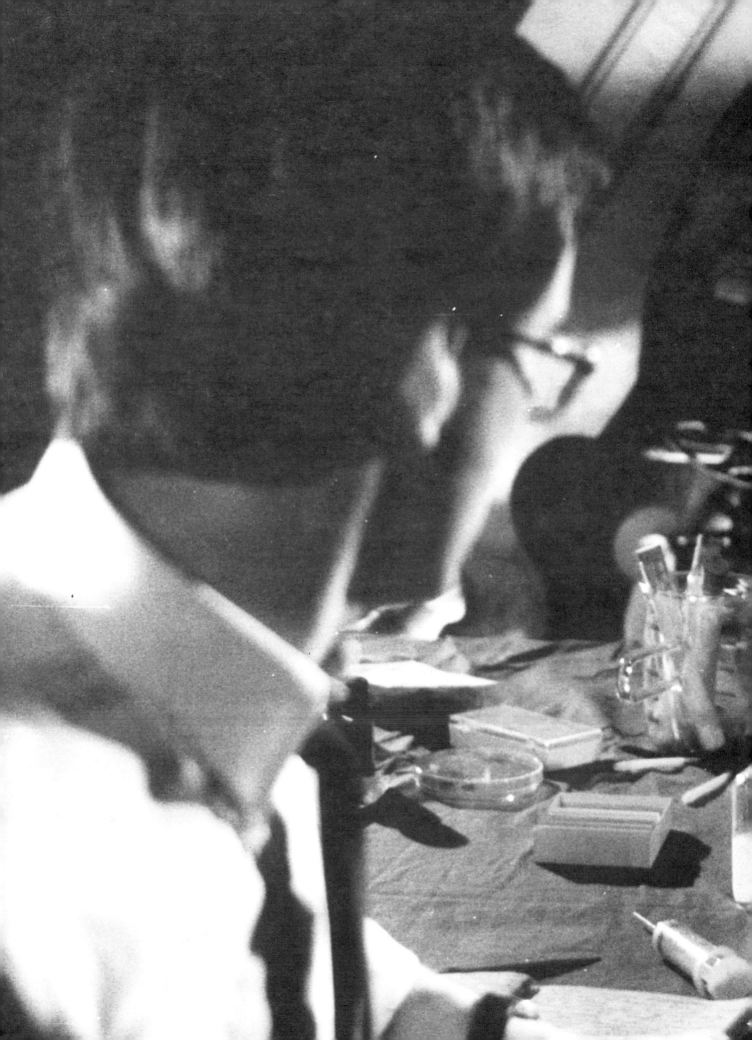

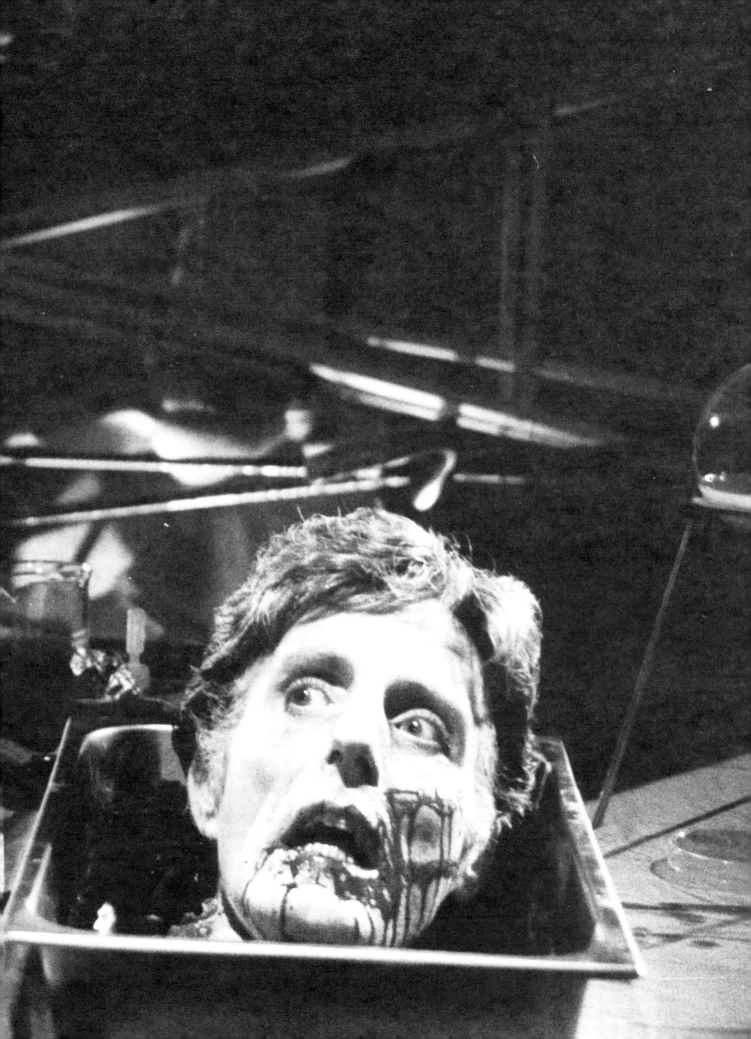

SCREAMING MAD GEORGE'S "SURREALISTIC" FX IN *Bride of RE-Animator* ARE STRICTLY AN ACQUIRED TASTE.

ing debut from Dave Parker, a long-time writer/editor/co-director at Full Moon Pictures and proved that, despite a dinky, hard-scrabble budget, this potent, hard-rocking zombie cocktail reflects nicely upon Parker's obvious affection and genuine respect for genre conventions. It also provides an illuminating glimpse into the bowels of guerrilla filmmaking, as Parker's film-within-a-film style explores the life and death risks of "shooting on a shoestring." Fortunately, Parker's savvy, knowledgeable approach puts every single dollar up there where it belongs—on the screen.

Mike Mendez' stylish and assured *The Convent* (2002) also displays the director's passion for the horror film; but also trots out a decidedly robust, anti-Catholic vibe—most likely fueled by an over-dose of forced "Hail Marys" recited during a misspent youth at Sister Theresa's School of a Thousand Sorrows. Adrienne Barbeau is fine, just superfine, as a leather-clad, cycle-riding avenging angel simply and masterfully blowing the fuck out of hordes of frothing, twitching, snarling zombie nuns from hell.

An expensive studio version of a popular video game, *Resident Evil (2002)*, was a cold, soulless souffle of computer-generated mayhem that proved as memorable as a rabid zombie dog's fart in a fierce tailwind.

Despite the time-proven resiliency of this sub-genre, certain films try their damnedest to derail this zombie train, either through careless neglect or outright incompetency, or misguided fervor.

KATHLEEN KINMONT GOES TO PIECES IN BRIAN YUZNA'S *Bride of Re-Animator.*

JEFFREY COMB'S VERY OWN BLOOD-SPLATTERED *Bride of Re-Animator.*

Pet Sematary II

Some are just homeless mutts with good intentions, desperately wanting to connect with just about anybody.

It's difficult to discern the reasoning behind Joel M. Reed's hair-raisingly stupid, toxic zombie snoozefest, *Night of the Zombies II (1981)*. Granted, it's arguably the first living dead film to feature a porno star stud working undercover for the CIA investigating a chemically-induced zombie plague somewhere in the Bavarian Alps, but puh-leeze! Self-reflective, politically correct deadheads who decry, "Zombies? We find that term...distasteful." Oh, blow me. The one and only shocking element in the whole fetid stew is that Reed was the direc-

tor of the notoriously fucked-up, titillating torture epic, *Bloodsucking Freaks (1978)*.

Zombie Island Massacre (1984) commits a very major *faux pas* for an undead flick—there are no goddamned zombies in the picture! The token "star" crawled to her 15-minutes of fame by being the wife of a disgraced Washington politician, clandestinely sucking his wazoo on the steps of Congress, then posing in a snarky *Playboy* spread to claim bragging rights. The horror...the horror.

Other dead flicks that begin to decompose right after the first reel were pretty easy to spot by their godforsaken titles alone: *Hard Rock Zombies (1984)*, *I Was a Teenage Zombie (1986)*, *I Was a*

Redneck Zombies IS A CAUTIONARY TALE WARNING OF THE HAZARDS OF BOTH
TOBACCO ABUSE AND THE OVER-CONSUMPTION OF TOXIC, RADIOACTIVE HOOCH.
BE CAREFUL, Y'ALL!

"REDNECK ZOMBIES, a back-woods blood-bath that'll tickle your funny bone, then rip it out!!" — Tim Ferrante, FANGORIA MAGAZINE

"A goremeister's delight... really delivers the 'goods'." — Dennis Daniel, DEEP RED MAGAZINE

LLOYD KAUFMAN and MICHAEL HERZ PRESENT A TROMA TEAM RELEASE

REDNECK ZOMBIES

Starring LISA DE HAVEN W.E. BENSON WILLIAM W. DECKER JAMES HOUSELY and TYRONE TAYLOR Original Soundtrack by ADRIAN BOND Director of Photography KEN DAVIS Production Design GEORGE SCOTT Edited by EDWARD BISHOP Produced by EDWARD BISHOP PERICLES LEWNES and GEORGE SCOTT Directed by PERICLES LEWNES

TOKEN PROTEIN. EDGE CITY. MERMIN

TROMA INC. FILMED IN ENTRAIL-VISION COLOR CAST PRODUCTIONS/FULL MOON PICTURES

WARNING:
REPEATED VIEWING OF REDNECK ZOMBIES HAS BEEN SHOWN TO CAUSE INSANE LAUGHTER IN LABORATORY ANIMALS.

Zombie for the F.B.I. (1986), *Zombie High* (1987), *The Video Dead* (1988), and the oh-so-cleverly titled *Chopper Chicks in Zombietown* (1991).

Armand Mastroantonio's *The Supernaturals* (1986) floundered when it tried to resurrect a zombie army of crusty-faced Confederate soldiers whose brief appearance during a climactic two minute graveyard disturbance failed to ignite a New Age Civil War.

Joe Piscopo, a former *Saturday Night Live* cast member turned musclebound potatohead, proved conclusively that the world was simply not yet ready for a zombie / buddy / cop / action / horror / comedy film when *Dead Heat* (1988) shit itself to death while in protective custody.

Despite the subgenre's wildly uneven output and its reliance on creaky, over-indulged convention, one group of aspiring filmmakers has never lost faith—the Backyard Zombie Massacre Auteur. Often made for less than the cost of a '64 Plymouth Valiant with a half-empty tank, these amateur dead-bangers are usually goofball vanity pieces—really heavy on the gore, and awfully light on story, characters, technique and Reason to Be. *Redneck Zombies* (1987); *Zombie Rampage* (1992), and *Zombie Cult Massacre* (1997) are undeniable labors of both love and hardheaded stubbornness; but perhaps only the latter can marginally claim some degree of distinction, simply because most of the makeup effects and gore inserts were created by cult auteur Jim (*Deadbeat at Dawn*, *Charlie's Family*) Van Bebber.

J.R. Bookwalter's *The Dead Next Door* (1989), reportedly one of the most expensive Super 8 features ever filmed, is a heartfelt, frothing fanboy tribute to *Dawn of the Dead* and also one of the most ambitious—supposedly co-financed by Sam Raimi (who later disowned it). Shot over a period of five years, Bookwalter's micro epic does showcase aerial shots of zombie attacks on both the (real) White House and Washington Monument, legions of the undead, cheeky black humor and superchunky gore. Other Raimi regulars participating during the long gestational period of the film include Bruce Campbell and Scott Spiegel.

Leif Jonker's *Darkness* (1993) is a self-assured, stylish Heartland Chunkblower that shows some real flair with its meaty and mannered handling during its numerous action set-pieces and rousing zombie attack sequences. Jonker displays an admirable grasp on the language of film and isn't at all hesitant when it comes to Painting the Town Red.

Is there any life left among the dead? Several wild and fearless foreign entries erupting on the cusp of the new millennium seem to provide an answer in the affirmative. These post-modern, Brave New Zombies prove, indeed, that once again, death is only the beginning.

Atsushia Muroga's *Junk* (1999), though technically polished and splashed through and through with an endearing, chunkblowing panache, proves so derivative it's damnably diverting. Besides borrowing heavily from such films as *Re-Animator*, *Day of the Dead*, *Zombie 3*, *Reservoir Dogs* and any number of John Woo shoot-'em-ups, some scenes appear to be lifted nearly intact and slavishly copied—using the same angles, lighting, camera moves and makeup styles. Which, of course, is not to say that it's without some downright stirring moments, including an army of the dead; splat-drenched Yakuza shoot-

BLOOD, BOOBS 'N' A LIGHT BITE: THE ABC'S OF *Redneck Zombies.*

outs; towering fountains of blood, chunks and assorted fluids; a naked, nubile zombie chick; and an applaudable use of a veritable shitstorm of maggots in a pivotal scene.

German director and well-credentialed gore-freak, Olaf Ittenbach, proved he could splash the sauce with the best of 'em with two earlier backyard splatfests, *Black Past (1989)* and *Burning Moon (1992)*, so it came as no real surprise that his first 16mm feature, *Premutos: Lord of the Dead (2000)*, rivals Peter Jackson's *Braindead* in sheer chunk-blowing excess. *Premutos* earns an easy "10" on the Gore Score even before the credit sequence concludes, and climaxes with a spinning Body Count-O-Meter that finally stops at "139," so you know all along just where this sick, demented slaughterthon is heading. It's marginally about a fallen angel and his vengeful band of the undead, and the battles they wage while skipping across the centuries, kicking ass and chopping, slicing, pounding, punching and pureeing the human form like only Olaf can. So many heads are sent to oblivion by shotguns; bodies bisected by chainsaws; and limbs removed by a variety of sharply bladed instruments in a welter of crimson gouts that it's...it's...nearly drowning in a pit of hi-calorie, chunky gorehound chili? Well, it's wet alright, but at times the stupidity level achieves near toxic totality. The annoying dialog is strictly cocktail chatter-light—it's padded with inane flashbacks, soccer footage and really cheesy opticals—and non-acted by a troop of butt-ugly brutes with really shitty teeth. But then, the drawn-and-quartered zombies; the cranial bisections; the machetes-in-the-mouth, and the secret zombie trick of a non-surgical penis removal technique will

win you over anyway.

Ittenbach's subsequent feature, *Legion of the Dead (2000)*, shot in 35mm with a workable budget, is far more polished, though just as downright idiotic; but of greater concern, of course, is the lack (by Olaf standards, anyway) of gratuitous, catastrophic gore. Again peopled by unlikeable morons spouting the most molar-grinding dialog imaginable, *Legion* spins a trio of parallel stories that intersect at an isolated desert diner, when a lanky, longhaired dude and his undead platoon mix it up with the locals. It proves a derivative, minimalist tale, though, combining elements from John Carpenter's *Vampires (1998)*, Richard Stanley's *Dust Devil (1993)*, and Robert Rodriguez' far, far superior *From Dusk 'Til Dawn (1996)*. Also tossed into the stew is a "genetic death virus," a plucky, zombie-killing waitress and endless shots of backlit guys in trenchcoats. Underwhelming... at best.

Tetsuro Takenchi's *Wild Zero (2000)* is a hyperkinetic take on zombies, UFOs, gangsters and rock & roll, that is as damnably entertaining as it is belligerently brainless. It's swaggering, slippery punk rock vibe is catalyzed by Guitar Wolf, a real three-piece band that plays a little like the Ramones, only ferociously out of tune. But Guitar Wolf is on the frontline when it comes to saving the world from flying saucers; zombies; Yakuza hardasses; evil gun dealers and fat dipshits wearing neon hot pants and sporting breathtakingly ugly haircuts. Despite the talky, walk-around tedium, seasoned heavily by some ice-pick-to-the-ears dialog and flamboyantly cheesy opticals, *Wild Zero* is a drunken, heady rush of cheap malt liquor and poppers, hot-wired by raucous raawwk songs with lyrics like "Exploding blood...roaring blood! Baby! Baby! Baby! Blood, blood, blood!" And, due to the fact that a certain epithet is used almost as often as in Brian DePalma's *Scarface*, you too can learn to say the "F-word" in Japanese. Though it exhibits little evidence of much brain-wave activity, your heart will surely be in your throat by the time our hero decimates an entire pack of zombies with flying guitar picks or splits a giant UFO down the middle with a samurai sword hidden in his six-string. There's also a tender, but simply cockeyed *Crying Game*-styled romance thrown in; but in the end, after quelling the zombie hordes and thwarting an interstellar invasion, our young couple learn a simple, but profound lesson: "Love has no borders, nationalities or genders." Golly.

Once again, guns, girls, gangsters and zombies figure prominently in Ryohei Kitamura's *Versus*

(2001), a wildly hyperkinetic amalgam of *The Matrix*, *Shogun Assassin*, *The Evil Dead* and John Woo flicks, that unwisely shoots its wad in the first reel. With a simple-minded, minimalist plot about an escaped prisoner's fateful meeting with the Yakuza and a mysterious girl in a haunted forest, director Kitamura turns his skills loose on a frenzied, jacked-up set of close encounters involving flashy swordplay, big-bang shootouts and massive bodily mayhem. These highly impressive sequences, all expertly staged and dazzingly shot, quickly reveal that the film has relatively no where to go with it. The action set-piece that sets the tone in the first reel is repeated often in an endless series of escalating variations on theme over the course of (a way too long) two hours. Kitamura's camera is all over the place: swirling 360-degree, DePalma-styled pans; hard charging, serpentine steadicam moves; and prowling,

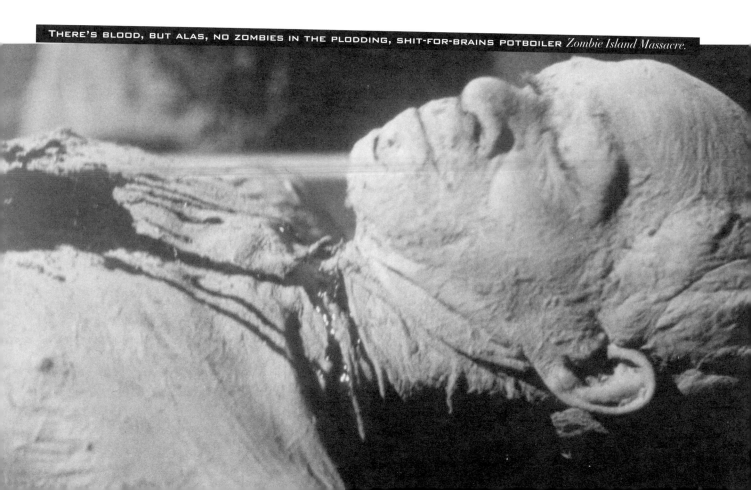

THERE'S BLOOD, BUT ALAS, NO ZOMBIES IN THE PLODDING, SHIT-FOR-BRAINS POTBOILER *Zombie Island Massacre*.

exploratory sweeps through bowling ball-sized holes punched in torsos. Essentially a plotless, exhaustively drawn out splatter/actioner set in a zombie-inhabited forest, *Versus* eventually delivers the goods, but it's a l-o-n-g and winding road.

Zombies have proven themselves to be a highly adaptable, resourceful and tenacious subspecies during their prolonged and torturous, 70-year quest to eat our guts. They have survived nearly everything thrown at them—death be not proud—and, though, perhaps they're not on screen quite as often now, they're still everywhere. Just look around. They're at your local shopping mall; behind the counters slopping chili cheese dogs at the Seven-Eleven; pushing stamps at the post office; validating your parking and ringing up the new Blink 182 CD at Tower Records. They even sit behind huge desks, take conference calls and network with their minions. Zombies no longer simply walk the earth—they run it.

And, somewhere back in Pittsburgh, George A. Romero is probably smiling.

FROM THE BOWELS OF THE EARTH THEY CAME....TO COLLECT THE LIVING!

CITY OF THE LIVING DEAD

EAGLE FILMS

CHARLES HAMM 1809-1847 R.I.P.

CHRISTOPHER GEORGE • KATHERINE MacCOLL • Directed by LUCIO FULCI

THIS FULCI ZOMBIE THRILLER WAS RELEASED STATESIDE AS *The Gates of Hell* AFTER GEORGE ROMERO COMPLAINED ABOUT THE ORIGINAL PROPOSED U.S. TITLE: *Twilight of the Dead.*

PINHEAD'S COUSIN, WIREFACE, *Hellbound: Hellraiser II.*

bLOOd REneGADeS

Without regularly-scheduled transfusions from a plethora of new blood donors, the horror film, arguably the most resilient, pliable and accommodating of all genres, begins a steady descent into repetition, irrelevance and self parody. This cycle signals the beginning of a kind of cinematic rigor mortis, to which the horror film is notoriously well suited. These cycles generally run in 15-to-17 year intervals and usually end with the audience laughing rather than screaming at the on-screen monstrosities. *Frankenstein (1931)* was a sublimely effective, classic frightfest; but 17 years and countless sequels later, the creature had been reduced to an impotent, buffoonish caricature, sharing the yucks and the one-liners with the stars in *Abbott and Costello Meet Frankenstein (1948)*.

Seventeen years after George A. Romero's seminal zombie noir classic, *Night of the Living Dead (1968)*, the genre again experienced an acute swelling and stiffening of the joints. The ground-breaking and fiercely uncompromised and controversial visions of stalwart directors, who'd helmed many of the previous decade's most riveting and unforgettable horror films, began to dim and lose focus. After three, four, or even five sequels and knockoffs, even the most unassailable classics will begin to decompose.

Halloween (1978) was an undeniable powerhouse shocker, a contemporary horror masterpiece and a box office cash cow. The first sequel, *Halloween II (1981)*, was already showing the strains of the plotline's inherent restrictions. The stalker formula was completely abandoned in *Halloween III (1982)*, but picked up again in 1988 for *The Return of Michael Myers*. By the time of *Halloween VI: The Curse of Michael Myers (1995)*, a once quintessential boogeyman became nothing more than an unwelcome, irritatingly lame joke.

Ofttimes, the directors themselves are fully cognizant of the genre's decline and the self paro-

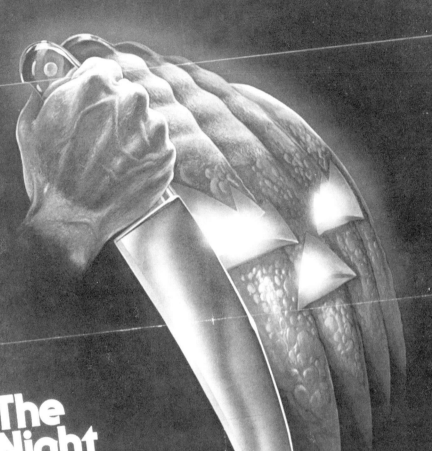

HALLOWEEN

The Night He Came Home!

MOUSTAPHA AKKAD PRESENTS DONALD PLEASENCE IN JOHN CARPENTER'S "HALLOWEEN"
WITH JAMIE LEE CURTIS, P.J. SOLES, NANCY LOOMIS · WRITTEN BY JOHN CARPENTER AND DEBRA HILL
EXECUTIVE PRODUCER IRWIN YABLANS · DIRECTED BY JOHN CARPENTER · PRODUCED BY DEBRA HILL
PANAVISION®   A COMPASS INTERNATIONAL RELEASE   R RESTRICTED

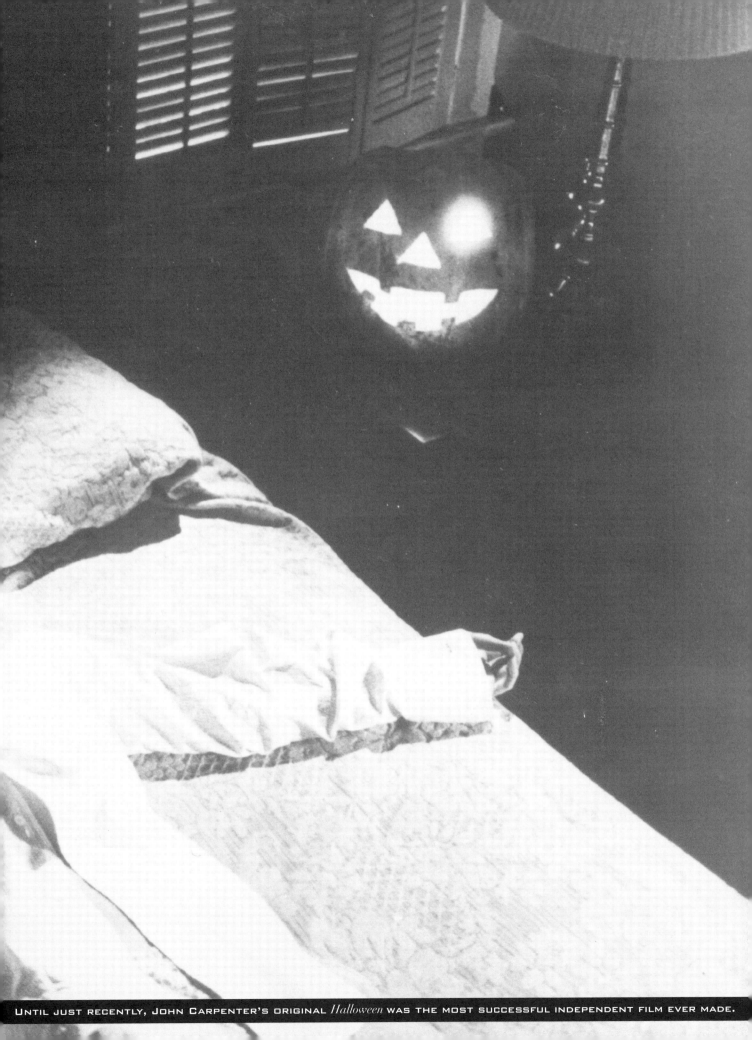

UNTIL JUST RECENTLY, JOHN CARPENTER'S ORIGINAL *Halloween* WAS THE MOST SUCCESSFUL INDEPENDENT FILM EVER MADE.

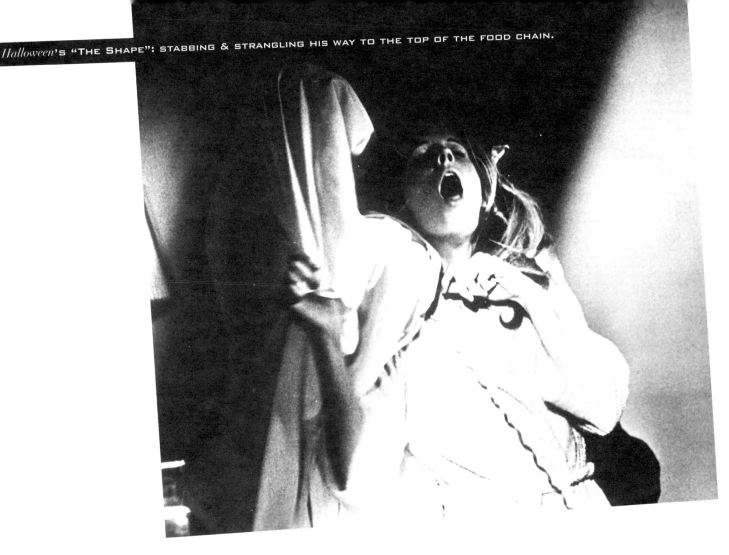

dy inherent in mindless repetition; but rather than attempt a remedy, they go for yet another repeat or a remake. When George Romero's casually and indifferently-scripted new *Night of the Living Dead (1990)* sucked zombie wazoo at the box office, the film threatened to become a metaphor for the entire genre. The dead were, indeed, among us. On the screen, behind the cameras and in the audience. Though Stuart Gordon's *Re-Animator (1985)* shone brightly and brilliantly, opening new doors to horrific exploration, few chose to follow. But soon, the worm was to turn...again.

Though sequels still appeared with alarming frequency and were apparently still providing enough of a financial incentive to insure their immediate survival, several new freshman directors were to break ranks and set the genre on its collective ear with an opening salvo of anarchic, taboo-breaking, revolutionary films of almost frightening diversity. Clive Barker's *Hellraiser (1987)*, John McNaughton's *Henry: Portrait of a Serial Killer (1986)*, Peter Jackson's *Bad Taste (1987)*, Jorg Buttgereit's *Nekromantik (1988)* and Jim Muro's *Street Trash (1987)* eclectically encompassed the latter's poster caveat: "Just when you had thought you'd seen it all." Though these films shared little in common, aside from the fact they all triumphantly bore the mark of a full-fledge auteur-in-action, they helped the genre reinvent itself yet again. And they showed others that Barker's wildly twisted, sado-masochistic credo

PREVIOUS PAGE
TOP: MICHAEL ROOKER'S INCENDIARY PERFORMANCE IN
Henry: Portrait of a Killer COULD PEEL THE PAINT RIGHT OFF YOUR WALL.

BOTTOM: HENRY'S PAL, OTIS, LOSES HIS HEAD OVER A GIRL.

ABOVE: *Rawhead Rex*

RIGHT: DESPITE THE AMBITIOUS AND SURREAL PLOTTINGS OF THE *Hellraiser* SEQUELS,
NONE COULD MATCH THE LEAN, MUSCULAR HORRORS OF BARKER'S ORIGINAL.

from *Hellraiser* — "There are no limits" — just might very well be true.

Clive Barker, an English playwright, painter and short story master, was just what the genre was aching for at the time his phenomenally successful literary series, *The Books of Blood*, was published in England in 1985. Barker was an intense, articulate, ferociously original talent whose cinematic visions were frighteningly surreal, unspeakably monstrous, sexually twisted and wildly amoral (all remaining absolutely essential to the plot, of course). Unfortunately, Barker had to perform beneath the auspicious shadow of Stephen King and the most inaccurate, misleading misquote of the decade that he was, indeed, "...the future of horror." He is not, was not, and

never will be; but Barker is clearly not afraid to take chances.

After expressing his contemptuous loathing of the screen treatment given two of his scripts, *Underworld (1985)* (aka *Transmutations*) and *Rawhead Rex (1986)*, Barker adapted a short story from his *Books of Blood*, "The Hellbound Heart," and directed *Hellraiser (1987)* as his debut feature. Incredibly imaginative, deeply provoking, alarmingly sadistic and skittishly uneven, the film introduced to wide-eyed and slack-jawed audiences the ethereal joys of systematic torture, flagellation, piercing and necrophilia. Barker had even flirted with the title *Sadomasochists from Beyond the Grave*, but was, no doubt, rebuffed by humorless studio sycophants equally afraid of that title's

THE DOCTOR IS...OUT OF HIS FUCKIN' MIND IN *Hellbound: Hellraiser II*.

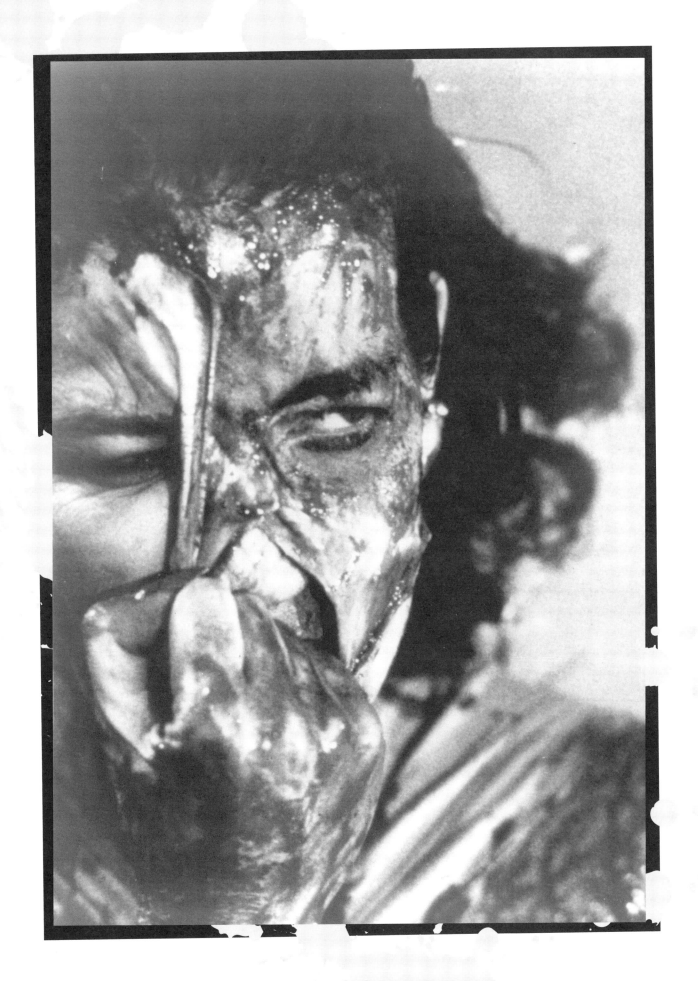

marquee value as well as Barker's unfettered and unapologetic celebration of the sexual proclivities of the dead and recently flayed.

Barker vacated the directorial chair for a pair of competent sequels, Tony Randel's *Hellbound: Hellraiser II (1988)* and Anthony Hickox's *Hellraiser III: Hell on Earth (1992)*, both of which showcased the endearing and compelling charms of one of Barker's most colorful and erudite denizens of the netherworld, the loquacious and enigmatic "Pinhead" (marvelously essayed by Doug Bradley).

Barker returned to direct *Nightbreed (1990)*, a critical and box office disappointment based on his novella *Cabal.* (Again, nervous executives balked at the original title, reportedly because no one knew what a "cabal" was.) The film featured a bewildered looking David Cronenberg (yep, that one) as a stocking-masked, button-eyed psycho slasher and a cadre of sensitive, misunderstood latex miscreants inhabiting the underground city of Midian. The film was dramatically cut and reedited by the studio, to Barker's chagrin, and to no one's gain. Barker also contributed to Bernard Rose's *Candyman (1992)*, an adaptation of Barker's urban boogeyman short story, "The Forbidden," as well as its sequel

THOUGH THE FILM WAS BASED ON CLIVE BARKER'S NOVELLA, *Cabal*, THE PRODUCERS CHANGED THE TITLE TO *Nightbreed* BECAUSE THEY FEARED THAT NO ONE KNEW WHAT A "CABAL" WAS.

Candyman: Farewell to the Flesh (1995).

While some high profile, highly anticipated projects fell through, including Universal's much touted *The Mummy*, Barker continued mining the literary vein with scattered success in a series of weighty, nearly-indecipherable "dark fantasy" tomes like *Weaveworld, Imajica, The Great and Secret Show* and *Everville*. His children's fantasy tale, *The Thief of Always*, was optioned by Stephen Spielberg's Amblin Enter-tainment and slated for future production as an animated feature.

In 1995, the stage was set for a major screen comeback as *Fangoria* magazine, the world's largest and most influential horror periodical, began a series of exhaustive articles detailing the day-to-day preproduction of Barker's supposed magnum opus *Lord of Illusions*. Based on a short story from volume six of *The Books of Blood*, "The Last Illusion," the film was hampered by numerous delays, reshoots and scheduling snafus. What emerged after a painful, all-too-public gestation period, was no masterpiece, but rather a flawed, though frequently brilliant, meandering epic that raised more questions than it answered about horror's Great White Hope. A tale of warring cult magicians whose

SAY MY NAME THREE TIMES IN THE MIRROR...
AND I'LL CURSE YOU WITH A TRIO OF *Candyman* SEQUELS.

stunts are not illusions, but real magic, the film forces the audience into a world of "rubber reality" where every slight misstep threatens the proceedings with total derailment. It is dangerous ground—what is real and that which is not, what constitutes magic and not fraud or trickery—and it is to Barker's credit that he maintains a precarious balance throughout until an underdeveloped climax nearly unravels the entire plot.

The books remain open in the strange case of Clive Barker. He has seemingly eschewed directing and feature film work to return to painting and writing, and maintains only a tangential relationship with the seemingly endless *Hellraiser*

series. He is clearly not the horror messiah many were expecting; but he is simply too talented, imaginative, ambitious and flamboyant to remain merely a footnote in the Future of Horror.

John McNaughton brought real horror back down to earth with his chilling *Henry: Portrait of a Serial Killer*, a no-budget masterpiece of brooding malevolence and sledgehammer intensity. Michael Rooker plays a violent, yet strangely appealing, wanton sociopath who tortures and murders people as if it were merely a messy, though necessary, part-time job for him. Though several of the murders are graphic, explicit and stomach churning, it is McNaughton's nonjudg-

212

NO, NO, VIRGINIA, HE DIDN'T GO THATAWAY.

The nasty bite of Tenefly Viper hooch. *Street Trash*.

DOWN THE TOILET, THE GAUDY, TECHNICOLOR TERRORS FROM *Street Trash*.

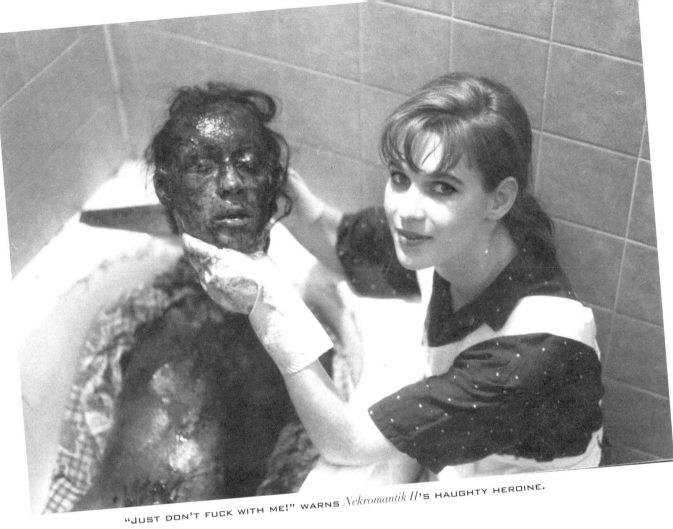

"JUST DON'T FUCK WITH ME!" WARNS *Nekromantik II*'S HAUGHTY HEROINE.

mental, *laissez-faire* approach to Henry's dementia that ultimately proves the most shocking. Shot in 16mm on the sly in Chicago for $111,000, *Henry* was loosely based on the supposed real-life exploits of world-class degenerate Henry Lee Lucas, who once boasted of close to 400 murders, but later recanted. When *Henry*'s producer, Steve Jones, once an associate of Stuart Gordon during his Organic Theatre days in Chicago, showed Gordon the film, the director gasped and admitted, "Makes what I've achieved on far bigger budgets look pitiful."

McNaughton's next project, budgeted at nearly 20 times that of his initial feature, was *The Borrower (1991)*, a tepid, sci-fi thriller about a body-hopping, decapitating alien that showed lit-

tle, if any, of the genius that made *Henry* live, breathe...and kill. McNaughton's next projects seemingly proved his foray into genre filmmaking was merely transitory. He directed a filmed version of Eric Bogosian's one-man show *Sex, Drugs, Rock & Roll (1991)*; teamed Robert DeNiro and Uma Thurman in *Mad Dog and Glory (1993)*; and helmed the raunchy, neo-noir sexcapade *Wild Things (1998)*.

Both Peter Jackson's *Bad Taste (1987)* and Jim Muro's *Street Trash (1987)* took splatter in a whole 'nother direction. In Jackson's case, a whole 'nother galaxy, where few dared go before. Both proved the critics wrong; the much-reviled, loathsome oxymoron "the horror comedy" was suddenly made almost respectable. Jackson's hilari-

Nekromanik's EVIL GENIUS—JORG BUTTGEREIT—AND FRIEND.

ously bent, gut-busting splatterfest featured big-assed aliens out to kidnap humans for use in an intergalactic burger chain. Muro's focus was on a voracious, bum-melting street toxin called "Tenafly Viper." Both were certifiable, first-class chunkblowers and as funny as the law allows: easily mixing the laughs with some of the most outrageous and over-the-top gore effects ever filmed. Jackson, a former postal worker in New Zealand, worked with a crew of friends for over four years (part-time and on weekends) on *Bad Taste*: acting, writing, directing, producing and handling the generous and meaty slate of special makeup FX. Jackson rapidly became the Orson Welles of Splatter Cinema, only it was *Citizen Carnage* this time and the key was Roseblood.

And lots of it.

Street Trash began life as a 20-minute student film and metamorphosed into a fully blown, 35mm tour-de-farce and gorefest extraordinaire that became a festival favorite (and winner of the Paris Festival Fantastique). If you never thought alcoholics, deranged Vietnam vets, multiple dismemberment, necrophilia, amputated penises, full-body meltdowns, spunk-licking canines or unsafe sex were funny before, you obviously haven't experienced the cinematic epiphany of *Street Trash*. Muro has yet to complete a second feature, opting instead for a big-buck career as one of Hollywood's most sought after steadicam operators (*Terminator 2*, *Seven*, *Heat*, *Red Dragon*).

Jackson followed *Bad Taste* with *Meet the*

PLEASE DO NOT TRY THIS AT HOME.

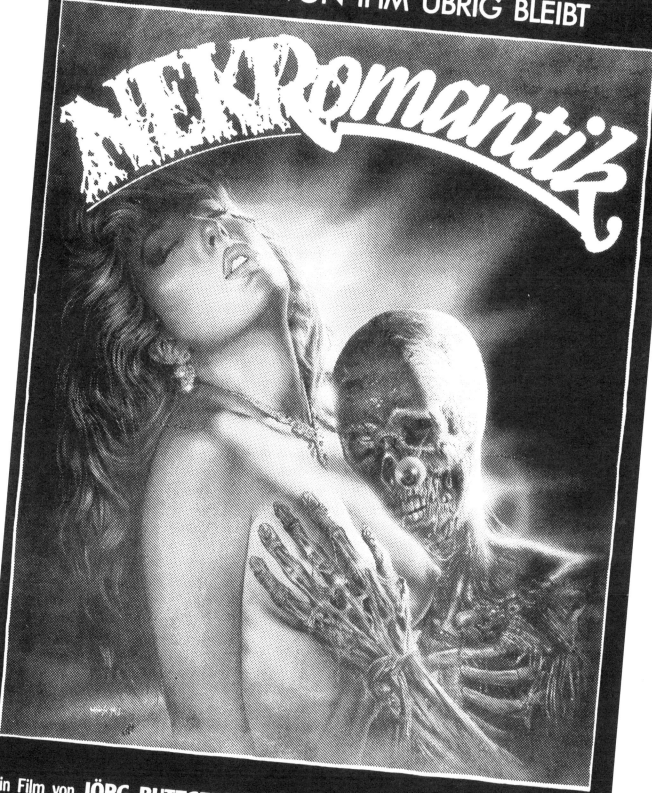

EIN FILM ÜBER DIE LIEBE ZUM MENSCHEN
UND WAS VON IHM ÜBRIG BLEIBT

NEKRomantik

Ein Film von **JÖRG BUTTGEREIT**

Produktion **MANFRED O. JELINSKI**

Feebles (1989), an eclectic Muppets Go To Hell scenario, featuring mostly non-human freakazoids involved in a plethora of perverse and disgusting puppet antics no sane person would ever want to witness. Therein lies part of Jackson's magic. He pushes, no pummels, the envelope into submission, creating entire new universes replete with their own operating manuals and their very own sense of sublime logic. He has the guts to never know when "enough is enough."

Meet the Feebles, a thoroughly original, totally unorthodox, uncompromising and belligerent feature, was also a very hard sell. Rejected by Southgate Entertainment (which had picked up the American rights) for its inflammatory content, the film languished for years, rarely seen and most frequently distributed only on Japanese import laser discs. Partially due to Jackson's future successes and newly-found political clout in the cinematic arena, *Meet the Feebles* was finally given the green light for a domestic distribution deal in 1996.

For his third feature, Jackson tackled his long-awaited tribute to both George Romero's *Dawn of the Dead* and the zombie subgenre and released what is inarguably the "Wettest Film Ever Made," *Braindead (1993)*. Because of copyright problems with a previous film of the exact same name directed by Adam Simon in 1989 and based on a 25-year-old screenplay by the late *Twilight Zone* scripter Charles Beaumont, Jackson's film was retitled *Dead Alive*.

Schramm HOPES THIS IS ONLY A DREAM...ONLY A DREAM.

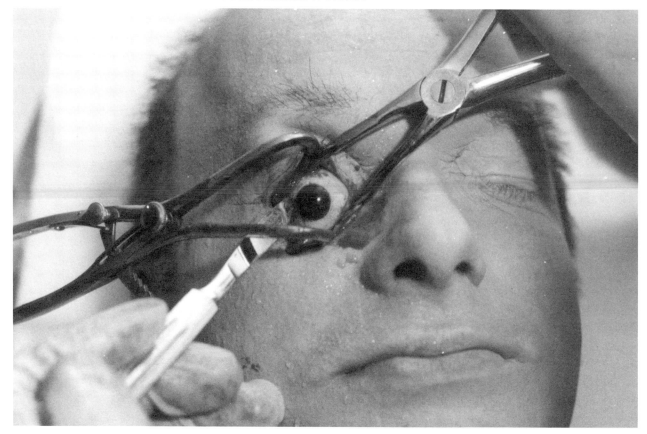

"..today I am dirty, but tomorrow I'll be just dirt"

SCHRAMM

MANFRED O. JELINSKI presents   a film by JÖRG BUTTGEREIT

starring FLORIAN KOERNER von GUSTORF MONIKA M MICHA BRENDEL CAROLINA HARNISCH
written by JÖRG BUTTGEREIT and FRANZ RODENKIRCHEN director of photography MANFRED O. JELINSKI
music by MAX MÜLLER and GUNDULA SCHMITZ special effects by MICHAEL ROMAHN

PRODUCED BY MANFRED O. JELINSKI   DIRECTED BY JÖRG BUTTGEREIT

THE GROPING GLOVE
TRICK IN THE SHOWER
ALWAYS GETS 'EM TO
APPRECIATE THE
Hardware.

THAT ENIGMATIC DESERT DUDE FROM RICHARD STANLEY'S SUPERLATIVE *Dust Devil.*

A zombie virus, spread by a Sumatran rat monkey, envelopes a country house, precipitating what could easily be the longest, most frenzied, sustained and satisfying chronicle of mass slaughter and meaty interpersonal mayhem ever attempted. The justifiably infamous, yet supremely cathartic, Toro Power Mower Massacre sequence proudly stands next to the "Parting of the Red Sea" from *The Ten Commandments (1956)* as an unassailable parcel of cinematic revelation. It's equal is not likely in our lifetimes.

Perhaps drenched to the marrow by the tidal wave of sauce spilled in *Dead Alive* and realizing he may well have made The Last Gore Film, Jackson retreated back to reality for once and co-wrote and directed his fourth feature (again with the aid of New Zealand Film Commission), *Heavenly Creatures (1994)*. Based on the real-life exploits of two dreamy-eyed, reclusive schoolgirls whose retreat into an insular fantasy world catalyzed the wrath of their parents an led to murder, *Heavenly Creatures* was internationally hailed by mainstream critics and rewarded by an Academy Award nomination for Best Screenplay. Jackson apparently bid a final farewell to hardcore horror by accepting the directorial chores on *The Frighteners*, a Michael J. Fox supernatural comedy-thriller released in 1996. Since Jackson's worldwide, mega-success with both *The Lord of the Rings: The Fellowship of the Ring (2001)* and *The Lord of the Rings: The Two Towers (2002)*, you'll never see his first three gore films ever show up on any of his newly revamped resumes. It's tough to let go of a towering talent like Jackson ("Pete, we hardly knew ye..."), but he left the horror world a banquet tableful of bloody and bodacious delights.

While many may eagerly anticipate what a favorite genre director may tackle in the future, one can only fear what German filmmaker and provocateur Jorg Buttgereit will do next. *Nekromantik (1988)* sent a jaded and complacent horror crowd reeling with its creepy, bleak and nihilistic take on modern romance, politics, sex and death. Fashioning a supremely disturbing *menage a trois* between two useless slackers and one very dead guy, Buttgereit assaults his audiences with such a bleak and deranged worldview that the suicide that climaxes the film easily becomes the only real and viable option available to those inhabiting his skewed and malevolent universe. Of course, it was no ordinary act of self termination. No, sirree. That's not quite how things work out in Buttgereit's master plan. There is pain and perversion. Skanky sex. Political putrescence. Loads of leering, desperate homunculi. Talk of death. Death. Then skanky sex...

A dramatic suicide has been employed as a plot device in literature, on stage, and in film for centuries. From the Bible to Shakespeare, Ibsen to Voltaire, from Arthur Miller to Buddy (*Combat Shock*) Giovinazzo, a well-timed act of self obliteration has always guaranteed an audience's rapt attention and heralded a radical turn of events. But it's nearly become as hoary a cliche as the terminal illness when used either indiscriminately or

desperately. In *Nekromantik*, Buttergeit uses the main character's climactic suicide as a kind of visual Drano; something with which to unclog stubborn receptor synapses before flushing them with an acid wash.

Spurned by his gal, unable to have sex with the living anymore, and losing interest in his job as a roadkill engineer, *Nekromantik*'s slimy anti-hero does what he has to do...with gargantuan gusto. Buttgereit doesn't blame the guy. After all, he did lose his girl and finish second to a putrefying corpse with a withered, Cheeto dick. Employing low-tech, samurai-style methods (no handguns—too fuckin' easy), The Doomed One continually plunges a long butcher knife into his stomach (in aching detail) until he notices he's become sexually aroused. He frees his frisky and bubbling boner just before expiring in a ceiling-splattering spray of blood and spunk. It is not a pretty sight.

But it thrust Buttgereit right onto the Splat Map, *muy pronto*, and became the underground buzz in dozens of fanzines for months after. It was easily the cinematic suicide *du jour* and served notice that more barricades were coming down...fast. Buttgereit also proved that with a vision (however skewed and thorny), passion, a Super 8mm camera and a swaggering sense of fearlessness you could flip a cinematic bird to all the world—and they would sit up and take notice.

The international notoriety of *Nekromantik* also provided a catalyst for other ultra low-budget auteurs who had become disenfranchised with the mainstream film business and wanted to experiment with riskier material. Buttgereit became a Punk Messiah to the legions of the underground and, much like the Sex Pistols, proved that you could, indeed, rock the world with two or three chords, a sneer and an attitude. Horror fans could now simply do-it-themselves, without restrictions, reservations or meddling from studio wazoos. They had to do it cheap, but they could do anything they wanted.

Soon, a flurry of Super 8 and video splatter flicks appeared, though most did nothing more than prove, indelibly, that Buttgereit's film was a total fluke. Many were made by fans without even an elementary understanding of cinema technique, screenplay structure, pacing or point-of-view. What they did know, however, was how to pump fake blood in firehouse gouts and by the gallon. The German-made, shot-on-video *Violent Shit* (1990) was a stellar, yet stinking, example of splatter fandom run amok. It was wet, alright, perhaps even one of the bloodiest films ever made; but it proved itself just another Gore Bore. Fans soon came to realize, many through personal experience behind the camera, that blood was merely a lubricant and punctuation to the process, not its *raison de etre*.

Other no-budget auteurs fared better, though. Nathan Schiff's *Long Island Cannibal Massacre* (1979); J. R. Bookwalter's *The Dead Next Door* (1989); Hugh Gallagher's *Goregasm* (1993); Leif Jonker's *Darkness* (1993); and Tim Ritter's *Killing Spree* (1987) and *Wicked Games* (1994) reinforced the notion that backyard splatter could still matter.

Jorg Buttgereit later graduated to 16mm film and followed with the inevitable sequel *Nekromantik 2* (1991). It, too, climaxes with a blood-soaked sequence of scurrilous sexual squalor nearly equal to the first. No mean feat, there,

ACID AGE HORRORS: VAN BEBBER'S *Charlie's Family.*

pardners. Buttgereit's other work, including *Hot Love (1991)*, *Der Todesking (1993)* (aka *The Death King*) and *Schramm (1994)* display a growing cinema sophistication with more complex storytelling, without sacrificing the razored-edge of his renegade approach to filmmaking. "I have to say," Buttgereit reveals, "that I'm not into horror films anymore, because there's nothing new in them... they're so boring! You know what's coming in advance. Nothing's exciting anymore." Buttgereit has forever changed all that by putting his money where his mouth is. And you probably don't even want to know where either that money or that mouth have been before.

Startling debut films from a couple of expatriates, now living and working in the United Kingdom, also contributed to the New Wave of Horror that began challenging the Stateside hammerlock on genre filmmaking. Richard Stanley, English by way of South Africa, and Mariano Baino, an Italian shooting films in both England and Russia, showcased their unique perspectives in two powerhouse debuts. Stanley's *Hardware (1990)*, a stylish, post-apocalyptic, cyperpunk spectacle, displays a cunning sense of humor and flirts with both the traditional and the anarchic in a tale of renegade cyborgs run amok. In a plague-ravaged futureworld, humans have become an endangered species as killer robots begin a lethal turn on their masters. Though Stanley's ambitious, eclectic and penetrating visual style reveals a world of astonishingly surreal sights and sounds, the film also embraces one of the most shopworn of all genre plottings: the Trap-Them-In-A-House-And-Let-The-Monsters-Get-'Em Syndrome. True, it is a great monster, a self-repli-

cating, conscienceless killing machine, and the heroine is a plucky, fetching resourceful type; but the suspense and tension are merely built on artifice and familiarity with similar situations exploited more effectively in both *Aliens* and the *Terminator* films. Stanley's original cut of the film was trimmed for its American release and lost a few seconds from some of its sex and splatter sequences, including a splashy, splendidly saucy elevator mashing (reminiscent of *Omen II*); but Stanley's hellish and provocative vision of a future dystopia remained fully intact.

Stanley's second feature, the frightfully ambitious, allegorical, quasi-metaphysical *Dust Devil (1991)* was filmed on location in South Africa and underwent a tortuous reediting process after the director delivered his original 120-minute cut. Stanley was clearly not amused. "My film is about suicide, magic and the devil in everyone," he explained. "It is all...magical reality. The demon operates inside dreams and can get to you when you're asleep."

The film's Stateside distributor, Mirimax Films, didn't quite see it that way. In their version, the film had to lose over 30 minutes of footage. "They cut it into a straight serial killer movie," Stanley has complained. "...They've left behind the magical content, making it merely baffling to U.S. audiences."

Stanley, a flamboyant, eccentric and unconventional personality to begin with, was to clash again with studio executives during pre-production of his next feature, a high profile, generously-budgeted remake of *The Island of Dr. Moreau (1996)*. He was summarily fired when his decidedly offbeat style collided with the demands made by

"EAT SHIT AND DIE, PIGS!" THE TWISTED SISTERS FROM
JIM VAN BEBBER'S PUNISHING MANSON OPUS, *Charlie's Family.*

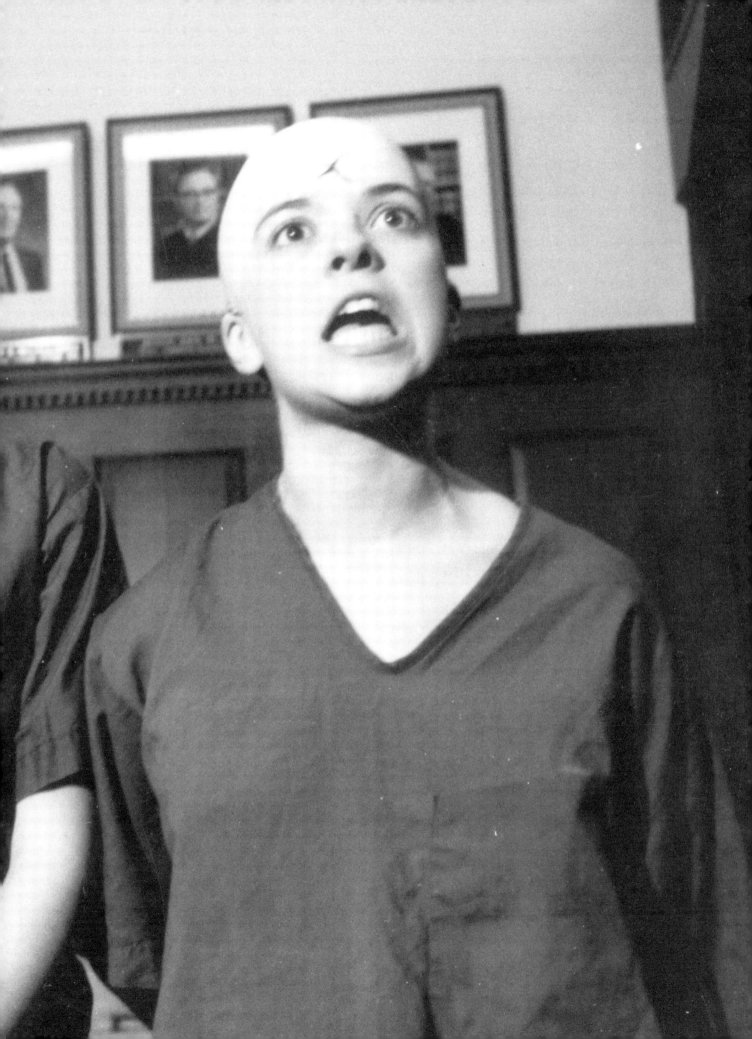

the film's male lead, a pricey Hollywood star unaccustomed to taking "no" for an answer.

Mariano Baino's 21-minute short—the wickedly seductive, gorgeously-photographed *Carancula (1991)*—was both a calling card and a homage to his spiritual mentor, Italian maestro Dario Argento. The film's shocking imagery, skewed camera angles, inventive lighting and supremely confident sense of purpose made this stylish, yet unsettling, film much more than merely a peek at one urban cannibal family's musings over their decidedly bizarre shopping list.

After securing financing from Russian, British and Italian sources, Baino journeyed to Tikraine and Crimea in the former Soviet Union to helm his first full-length feature, *Dark Waters (1994)*.

"I want a horror movie to be scary and grievous," Baino has stated. "It must provoke fear and anxiety. I just can't stand comic horror movies. I hate seeing a murderer who kills his victims and then offers a wisecrack so the spectators can relax and have a laugh."

For a young man who claims the Bible is probably, "the best horror novel ever written," these are potent observations. *Dark Waters* is filled with Baino's brooding obsessions with evil, sin, salvation, childhood trauma and religious iconography. While slow and sluggish at times, the film, nonetheless, explores a troubling and challenging moral terrain rarely visited by today's formulaic genre hacks. Clearly, Baino's reach still slightly exceeds his grasp; but that promises to change swiftly by his sophomore feature, *Ritual*, a Graham Masterton story about cannibalism and twisted religion. It's also highly refreshing and encouraging to know of another young filmmaker who's just as bored by teenage bodycount epics as the rest of us.

Jim Van Bebber, a Dayton, Ohio filmmaker, writer, actor, stuntman and effects artist, may be one of the very best new directors you've never heard of. A well-kept underground secret that threatens to go ballistic with the imminent release of his lifelong opus, *Charlie's Family*, Van Bebber is a rugged, fiercely passionate, no-nonsense visionary whose previous work has earned him various festival awards and a stellar, unimpeachable cult reputation. A former film student at Wright State University, Van Bebber has crafted several short films of undeniable power and presence. His 1993 effort, *My Sweet Satan*, was the recipient of the Grand Prize at the New York Underground Film Festival.

Roadkill: The Last Days of John Martin (1988) is a punishing, abrasive, day-in-the-life of a beer-swilling, varmint-scarfing, monosyllabic sociopath who decides people are far more fun to hunt than oppossums. Martin lives in a rat-infested, puke-flecked shithole, decorated with human skin masks and littered with animal carcasses. He frequently converses with his blaring TV set and likes to build little chicken wire crematoriums atop his gas stove. One of his last days is spent dismembering and beheading one hitchhiker and flame broiling the other.

Deadbeat at Dawn (1988) was Van Bebber's first full-length feature, a gritty, violent and palpably exciting descent into the turf wars brewing between a couple of brutal street gangs. Van Bebber also wrote the screenplay, edited the film, performed the stunts, handled the gory FX and starred as one of the gang leaders. The film cli-

Dark Waters

maxes with a well-choreographed street fight ending in a wincingly vicious knifing that provides one of the most ghastly and downright depressing finales since Buddy Giovinazzo's *American Nightmares (1986)* (aka *Combat Shock*).

My Sweet Satan (1993) was Van Bebber's hellish vision of a real-life murder case involving a small-time, drug-dealing thug who's also a part-time Satanist. When the dealer is ripped off by one of his weaselly minions, Ricky (played by Van Bebber with a positively hair-raising veracity) schemes for payback during an acid-drenched campfire sequence guaranteed to split your skull. After the perpetrator is bounced around and repeatedly humiliated by Ricky and his partner, the ugly knives come out. In a stabbing sequence of unparalleled fury (that is, until *Charlie's Family* came along), the victim is left bleeding and squealing until his head is mashed into a crunchy jello souffle by two pair of Doc Martens. The film ends with the imprisoned Ricky wrapping a sheet around his neck and hanging himself in his cell. There are no victors and no mercy in Van Bebber's woeful world. Everyone always loses.

Charlie's Family (2003) took over ten years to complete, filming on weekends, nights, and anytime Van Bebber could scrounge up enough money to secure another can of film. It is a very troubling and very intense masterpiece of *cinema verite*, a scalding and ferociously courageous debunking of the Charles Manson Mythos that make previous Manson epics look like Cub Scout hootenannies.

Told in mock documentary style and employing a fictionalized television producer who's assembling footage for a special on "the Family" for the 25th anniversary of the Tate-La Bianca murders, *Charlie's Family* never flinches, never blinks and never gives an inch. It is a harrowing, debilitating, fearsome journey into a bleak, amoral landscape, populated by soul-less scavengers bound by blood to a messianic mad dog. The Shorty Shea and La Bianca murders are shorn of all cinematic artifice and presented with all the panache and appeal of a real snuff film. The Tate house massacre is even worse—Van Bebber really did his homework here—as nearly every one of Voytek Frykowski's 51 stab wounds are presented in vivid, horribly graphic detail. Mercifully, and out of a "profound respect for her husband, Roman Polanski," explained Van Bebber, the Sharon Tate murder is not dwelled upon. Be thankful for small favors. *Charlie's Family* is an incendiary, devastating and deeply disturbing glimpse into the Belly of the Beast. No prisoners are taken. No mercy is asked. It is no venal entertainment, but a horrifying epiphany of the highest order.

As a new century of filmmaking begins, the horror film continues to eclectically explore all of the ever-changing faces of fear. There no longer seems to be any discernible pattern emerging either. We have: hi-tech; low-tech; horror/sci-fi; the supernatural; big bugs; little bugs; wiseass aliens; backyard witches and surrealistic splatter. Not to mention of course, the zombies, psychos, demon nuns and roadside cannibals that are still major players in the Game of Gore.

So, we'll be hearing more, much more, from these freshly-recruited, New Blood Renegades: Rob (*House of 1000 Corpses*) Zombie; Guillermo (*Cronos*, *Mimic*) del Toro; Mike (*The Convent*) Mendez; Dave (*The Dead Hate the Living!*) Parker; Dante (*Desecration*, *Horror*) Tomaselli, and Olaf (*Premutos: Lord of the Dead*) Ittenbach.

The future of fright seems in good hands.

INDEX

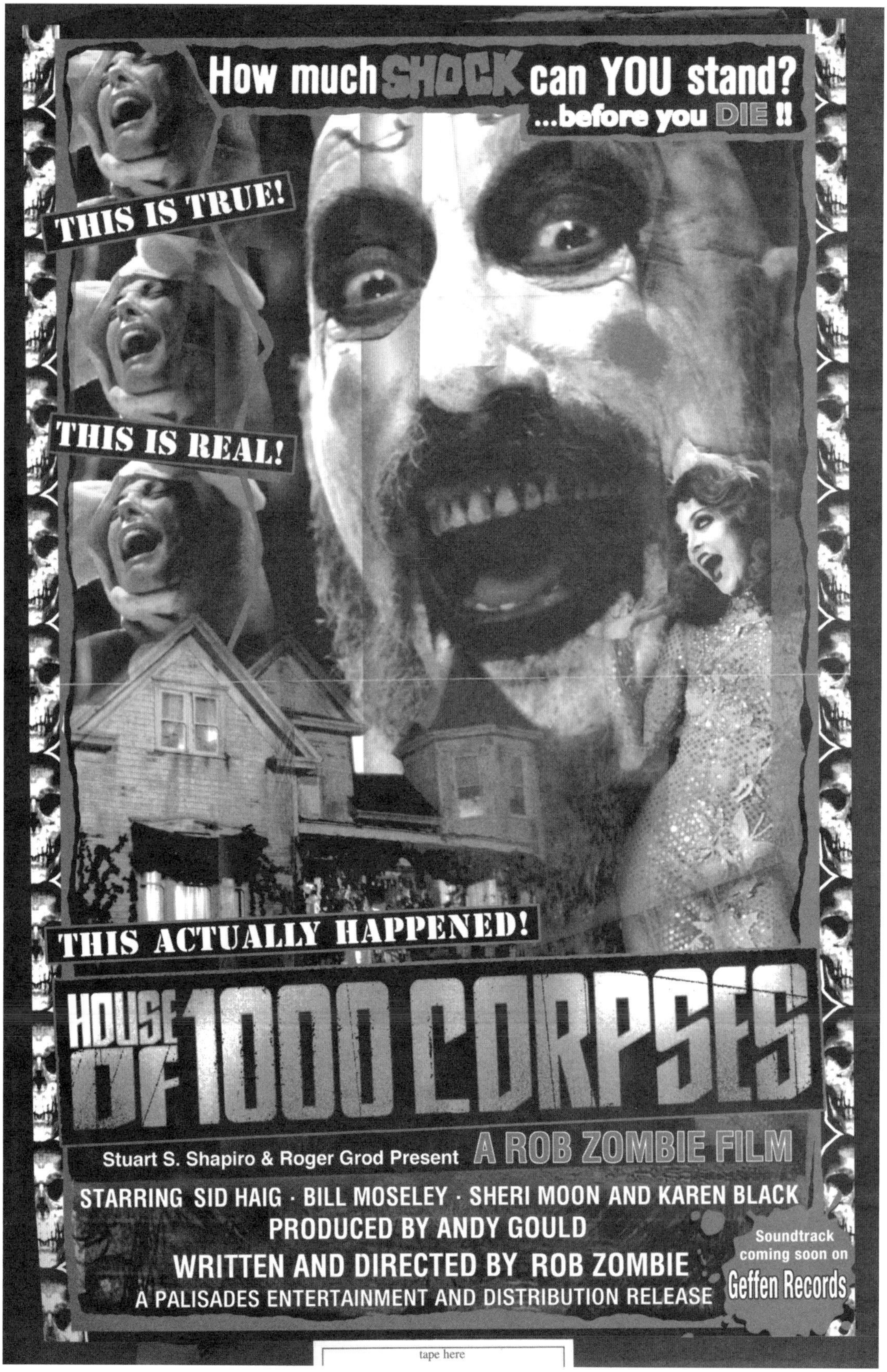
How much SHOCK can YOU stand?
...before you DIE !!
THIS IS TRUE!
THIS IS REAL!
THIS ACTUALLY HAPPENED!
HOUSE OF 1000 CORPSES
Stuart S. Shapiro & Roger Grod Present
A ROB ZOMBIE FILM
STARRING SID HAIG · BILL MOSELEY · SHERI MOON AND KAREN BLACK
PRODUCED BY ANDY GOULD
WRITTEN AND DIRECTED BY ROB ZOMBIE
A PALISADES ENTERTAINMENT AND DISTRIBUTION RELEASE
Soundtrack coming soon on
Geffen Records

tape here

aBOut ThE AUthoR

Chas. Balun is a native Californian and a seasoned cult writer and horror film fanatic who has actually seen the original *Texas Chainsaw Massacre* over 25 times since its initial release. Balun is an indisputable horror film fan and a strong voice behind the genre, and has been associated with the genre for several decades. Chas. has spilt ink (as a contributor) for *Fangoria* (the world's leading horror movie magazine) and *Gorezone*, and currently serves as the founding editor of *Deep Red* (a cult magazine devoted to splatter horror movies). Balun has also authored several books about horror films including the original 1986 *Horror Holocaust*, *The Connoisseur's Guide to the Contermporay Horror Film*, *Gore Score*, *More Gore Score*, *Gore Score 2001: The Splatter Years* and *Lucio Fulci: Beyond the Gates* as well as the kick-ass novel *Ninth and Hell Street*. His novella, *Director's Cut* has been optioned by filmmaker Stuart (*Re-Animator*) Gordon for a future film project. Balun was the Creature Designer for Fred Olen Ray's feature film, *Evil Toons*, and a storyboard artist for the award-winning Smithsonian IMAX film *To Fly*. Chas. Balun can also be seen on Showtimes' *Masters of Horrors* shock-u-mentary along with the likes of George Romero, Wes Craven, John Carpenter and other horror movie luminaries. Balun also appeared in the Brian Yuzna film *Society*. He is a professional illustrator and graphic designer and the art director for Rotten Cotton Graphics (see Rottencotten.com). Balun admits that he still has a special place in his heart for the film, *Ring of Bright Water* — go figure!